George Booth

Maryland Line Confederate Soldiers' Home

Illustrated souvenir

George Booth

Maryland Line Confederate Soldiers' Home
Illustrated souvenir

ISBN/EAN: 9783337136086

Printed in Europe, USA, Canada, Australia, Japan

Cover: Foto ©Andreas Hilbeck / pixelio.de

More available books at **www.hansebooks.com**

ILLUSTRATED SOUVENIR

Maryland Line

Confederate Soldiers'
Home,

PIKESVILLE, MARYLAND.

COMPILED BY

CAPT. GEO. W. BOOTH,

PUBLISHED IN THE INTEREST OF AND UNDER THE SUPERVISION OF
THE BOARD OF GOVERNORS AND MANAGERS
OF THE HOME.

1894.

Visitors to the Home—Take the Druid Hill Avenue (yellow) Cable cars; Gilmor Street (red) Cable cars, and Carey Street (white) Electric cars, which connect with PIKESVILLE Electric cars at Retreat Street, direct to Main Entrance of the Home.

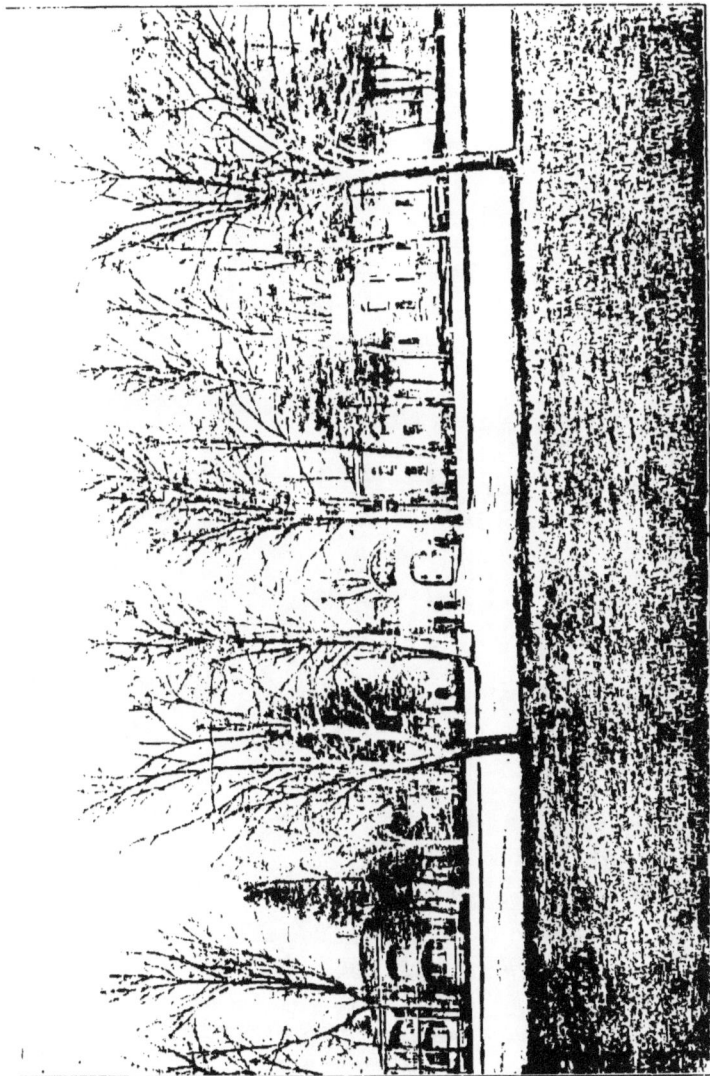

MARYLAND LINE, CONFEDERATE SOLDIERS' HOME, PIKESVILLE.

FORM OF BEQUEST OR, DEVISE TO THE MARYLAND LINE
CONFEDERATE SOLDIERS' HOME.

I bequeath, or devise to the Association of the
Maryland Line. of Baltimore City. Maryland

For the Support of the Maryland Line Confederate
Soldiers' Home.

Witness

Witness

If Money is left, the proper word is "*bequeath*"; if Real Estate,
"*devise*" is the term.

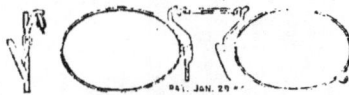

Harris' Academy of Music.

Mrs. P. HARRIS,   R. L. BRITTON,   TUNIS F. DEAN,
PROPRIETORS AND MANAGERS.

The most perfectly equipped Temple of Amusement in the United States. The best ventilated Theatre in Baltimore. Pure atmosphere. The entire edifice lighted by the Fort Wayne Electric Co.—2,200 16-candle-power lamps. On the ground floor. Over 50 exits leading direct to the street. The same scale of prices always prevails. Seating capacity 3,000. The lowest insurance rate of any theatrical structure in the city. Convenient access to all car lines in the city.

1774.

Perfection
in
Flour.

1894.

The Premier
Flour
of America.

JOHN G. HETZELL & SON,
Metallic Roofing and Spouting,

Copper and Galvanized Iron Cornices, &c.

MADE ACCORDING TO ARCHITECTS' DRAWINGS.

Also Hayes' Patent Ventilating Fire-Proof Skylights, Conservatories, and other Glazed Structures, Ventilators and Chimney Caps, Corrugated Iron Roofing, Siding and Ceilings, and Dealers in Tin Plate, Zinc, Galvanized Iron, etc.

ROOFS PAINTED.   ALL WORK WARRANTED.

No. 225 North Howard street,

Telephone No 1131.   **BALTIMORE.**

J. P. Steinbach, IMPORTER & TAILOR,
EQUITABLE BUILDING.

119 EAST FAYETTE STREET.

ASSOCIATION OF THE MARYLAND LINE.

MARYLAND LINE

CONFEDERATE SOLDIERS' HOME.

THAT there was a division of sentiment in Maryland, upon the causes which led to the war between the States, no one will deny ; yet no intelligent observer, or one at all familiar with the facts, will refuse to admit that the large preponderance of public opinion was heartily in favor of the cause of the South.

Maryland, by reason of her geographical location, close commercial interests with the Tobacco and Cotton-raising States, similarity of institutions and intimate social and natural relations with the people south of the Potomac, was emphatically a Southern State, notwithstanding it had come to be classed with that division of the country lying north of the Potomac and south of New England, called the Middle States. Of the same ancestry, prevailing customs and habits, and kept closely welded by intermarriage, together with the memories of the past struggle of the Colonies in the French and Indian Wars, and of the free and independent States which determined to throw off allegiance to Great Britain and King George—with the same views of the character of the Federal Union, and the rights and privileges which were reserved to the States under the Constitution of 1789, it would have been unnatural to have found her people engaging in a fratricidal war of desolation and invasion of those communities, to which she was so bound by historic and sympathetic ties.

The conservatism of her people misled some to indulge the hope that what was popularly called the "love of the Union" would overcome the considerations of honor and the association of years of common struggle and danger ; but such conceptions were as unfounded as they were insulting to the manhood and integrity of her people. The right of self-government had, on this Continent, no firmer supporters and defenders than in Maryland. It did not take long to make manifest the temper and intentions of her people ; and, therefore, by the strong arm of power, and by a most vigorous military despotism, were her legislative bodies dissolved, her leading citizens jailed and sent to dungeons, and the condition of the State reduced to that of an alien principality held by armed forces. The blow fell no less quickly than it did firmly; but still it did not prevent the young men of the Commonwealth from forsaking the comforts of their homes, and singly, or in small parties, crossing the Po-

tomac and enlisting in the Armies of the Confederacy, to battle for the rights of their State, even though she was manacled and helpless. Unable to speak for herself through the regularly appointed methods, the sovereignty of Maryland found representation in the strong arms of the fifteen thousand or more- the flower of her youth, who gave their service to the South, and in the anxious hearts of those who remained at home, and nightly sent up their blessings and prayers for the absent ones, while their daily care was to mercifully assist the unfortunate who, in prison, and hospital, was visited and ministered unto, as far as the sufferance of those in power would permit.

The devotion of the women of Maryland, and the insult and indignity to which they were subjected in these merciful ministrations, are of the past ; but no less will the truth of history chronicle their deeds and the oppression under which her people lived during the dreary years of the war. Allusion is only made to these circumstances to explain why it is that we have here in Maryland- a State that was not " out of the Union" —a home for Confederate soldiers. Her sons were in the Confederacy ; the hearts of her women were there, and the great body of her people were in sympathy with the cause of constitutional government, with regard to the reserved rights of the States, according to the spirit of the Constitution, and opposed to the action of the Federal Authorities in the purpose to coerce the States of the South, who were asserting this right.

As a border community in a sectional quarrel, this feeling could not be unanimous. There were some who were loyal to the Union, and this minority, obtaining control by reason of the bayonets of the Federal power, gave the weight of State authority to their claims, and we find Maryland regiments and Maryland batteries (Maryland at least in name,) responding to the call of the Federal President. The muster rolls of these organizations, in the archives of the State, are not conclusive as evidencing the true feeling of her people. It is conceded that there were those who honestly supported the National authority, and the brilliant record of Maryland soldiers who " wore the blue," is cherished and prized as the common glory of the State, by none more dearly than those of her sons who " wore the grey," and followed the banners of the Confederacy, but they do not admit that the former were the exponents of the great heart of Maryland.

As in the days of the Stuarts, the hearts of the loyalists were " o'er the water with Charlie," so was it in Maryland. Her body bound and shackeled, her heart was unchained, and her sympathies were with the followers of Lee and Jackson, beyond the Potomac.

The representation of Maryland in the Southern armies has been variously estimated--there are no positive data to determine the fact. They were found scattered throughout the entire army, in almost every organization and command. This will be understood when it is remembered that only as individuals they could make their way through the lines, and make good their passage to the Confederacy. Many in this way attached themselves to the first Confederate command they met ; others sought out old friends, or, perhaps, family connections, and enlisted in the same command with their relatives or friends. A prominent

officer, after inspection of the records of the office of the Adjutant-General of the army in Richmond, estimated that there were twenty thousand Marylanders in the service of the Confederate States. The organizations officially recognized as from Maryland were as follows :

FIRST MARYLAND INFANTRY,
SECOND MARYLAND INFANTRY,
FIRST MARYLAND CAVALRY,
SECOND MARYLAND CAVALRY,
FIRST MARYLAND ARTILLERY (Andrews and Dement),
SECOND MARYLAND ARTILLERY (Baltimore Light),
THIRD MARYLAND ARTILLERY (Latrobe),
FOURTH MARYLAND ARTILLERY (Chesapeake).

The above composed the Maryland Line, and were recognized as such by the Confederate authorities. Their aggregate strength was some four thousand men. It is not within the province of this paper to give the brilliant history and record of these organizations. With the exception of the 3rd Maryland Artillery, which served with distinguished honor with the army in the West, it is enough to say, in the language of General Ewell, referring to the First Maryland Infantry : "The history of the First Maryland Infantry is the history of the Valley campaign ;" the history of the Army of Northern Virginia cannot be written without giving the history of these commands of the Maryland Line. From the early days of the war—from Manassas to Malvern Hill,—from the Valley to Gettysburg,—from the defense of Petersburg to Appomattox—was their valor and efficiency conspicuous. The general orders and reports of the various commanders under whom they served—Johnston, Jackson, Ewell, Stuart, Fitz. Lee, Hampton, and the illustrious commander, General Robert E. Lee, are uniform in their praise as soldiers, worthy successors of the "Maccaronies," who, under Smallwood and Gist, on Long Island, held back the British advance and made such heroic sacrifices, while Washington was enabled to withdraw in safety ; and of the Continentals who, with DeKalb at Camden, preserved the honor of the American arms, or who, under Williams and Howard, made possible the after successes of Greene in the Southern campaign.

From the beginning at Harper's Ferry, in '61, to the end at Appomattox, in '65, they maintained the same high character and bearing, and the record of their deeds, the reputation of their Commanders—of Buchanan and Hollins, of Trimble, Elzey, Winder, Steuart, Johnson, Herbert, Ridgley Brown, Gilmor, Andrews, Wm. Brown, and Breathed, are held in veneration and affection by all familiar with the military history of the Confederacy, and have made for Maryland a name equal if not above other names in the admiration of a heroic people.

The State of Maryland can well be proud of its sons of the Maryland Line of 1861–1865, as it has always been of their forefathers of the Revolution and the subsequent wars of 1812 and with Mexico ; and it is but fitting that this feeling of satisfaction should take sensible form in providing for its survivors who, outliving the times of their heroic effort, had at last been made to fall victims of the relentless advances of increas-

George Brehm's

CELEBRATED

B E E R

BREWERY: BELAIR AVENUE.

◆◆◆◆◆◆◆

ONE   GRADE   ONLY.

GENERAL BRADLEY T. JOHNSON, *President.*

MAIN ENTRANCE.

ing years and dire poverty, or, perhaps, disabled by wounds received in battle. An honorable, brave people are never forgetful of their veteran soldiers, and the fact that the Federal Government has so generously provided for those of her sons who wore the blue, but makes more pronounced the obligation of our Mother State to care for their unfortunate brothers who, in ragged grey jackets, represented her in the Confederate ranks ; and, to their honor be it said, in this pious purpose the Union citizens of the State have been willing and earnest in their co-operation.

SAD INDEED was the heart of the poor Maryland Confederate, after the days of Appomattox—the cause to which he had devoted his best years, and for which he had so freely risked his life and shed his blood, had failed,—as the tearful good-bye was spoken to his associates, memories of the comrades who had yielded up their lives during the great struggle, came to him; they happily needed no parole to give them immunity or protection. In the great beyond they had found a rest and a home. The toils of the march, the privations of the camp, and the dangers of the field were over, and with a mighty wail of suffering anguish, the heart of the Confederacy was broken. Like Marius, he gazed on the ruins, as it were, alone ; for, whither should he now turn ? There was a very mockery in the terms of his parole—" permission to return to his home ;" where was that home? The vindictive feeling that was then ascendant, denied him refuge in the land of his birth, and he was forced to patiently await the ebb of passion and the return of reason. This change was not long coming, and the joys of meeting with loved ones, soothed his wounded heart and gave him fresh courage to meet the stern realities of the hour. Not given over to futile repinings, or idle sorrow, he realized the duties of the present, while not forgetful of the glories of the past, and earnestly engaged in the battle for livlihood—no less fierce than those through which he had recently passed. As his position became assured, although the cares which pressed upon him were severe and trying, he found time to keep up the association of comrades, and determined on an effort to keep fresh the memories of the dead, to assist the disabled and the destitute, and to preserve for posterity a true account of the great struggle and the motives which led him to take up arms. Submitting to the arbitrament of the sword, he appealed to the impartial judgment of the future to justify his past.

The Association of the Maryland Line was formed in 1880, with these objects in view. There was already in existence the Society of the Army and Navy of the Confederate States in Maryland, which was organized in 1871, shortly after the death of General Lee, and it was not proposed to encroach upon, or to displace this organization, but still to cherish it as the parent society, or centre of Confederate influence and work. Under the direction of General Bradley T. Johnson, and largely aided by his material assistance, the Association of the Maryland Line made up a fairly complete roster of the various Maryland organizations. In this work they were largely aided by the courtesy of the War Department, in permitting access to such muster rolls as were found in the records of the Adjutant-General's office at Richmond, and which were removed to Washington at the close of the war.

Under the auspices of the Society of the Army and Navy of the Confederate States in Maryland, was held in Baltimore in 1885, a most successful bazaar, the proceeds of which, some $31,000, were being devoted to the care of indigent Confederates and the burial of the dead. Through the medium of this fund, and the contributions of generous friends, the duty of ministering to the wants of the unfortunate was faithfully performed, but as the years rolled on it became painfully apparent that the means at hand were not equal to the emergency, and that the applications for assistance were far beyond the ability to meet. It was soon developed that a number of these gallant old soldiers were finding refuge in the alms houses of the State, and not a few instances came to light of the burial of dead in the unhallowed graves of Potter's Fields. After careful consideration, and appropriate methods for engaging public attention, it was suggested to make an attempt to raise an amount of money sufficient to build a cottage at the Richmond, Va. Home, to which these destitute veterans could be sent, and to appeal to the General Assembly for proper financial or other aid. This proposition was earnestly canvassed, and after mature deliberation, it was determined to make an effort to establish a Soldiers' Home in Maryland, and to ask that the property known as the Pikesville Arsenal be devoted to that purpose. To this memorial the General Assembly gave ready ear and took prompt affirmative action, and in February, 1888, the above mentioned property was given by the State to the Association of the Maryland Line, for the purpose indicated, and an appropriation of $5000 per annum was at the same time voted for the repair of the property and maintenance of the Home. This property was singularly adapted to the purpose, by reason of the character of the buildings and convenience of location. The ravages of time and abandonment had, however, sadly marred its fair proportions, and large expenditures were necessary for its rehabiliment. In this connection, it may be interesting to give the history of the establishment of this post, outlining the purposes sought to be accomplished by its location, etc. The following report by Lieut. Baden, dated U. S. Arsenal, May 23rd, 1823, is in the possession of the Home, having been furnished by the War Department in connection with a plat of the property, shortly after the transfer of the same by the State of Maryland to the Association of the Maryland Line.

UNITED STATES ARSENAL, near Baltimore.

"I will here endeavor to develop in as clear and concise a manner as possible, what I conceive to have been the object of the Government in the erection of this establishment, and its capacity to fulfill the purposes for which it was constructed:

"First. It was clearly perceived at the commencement of the late war with Great Britain, that our great commercial cities on this seaboard would be proper objects of attack by the enemy, and in many instances would be greatly exposed. Baltimore appears to have been particularly chosen as an object of attack, and from the great extent of the waters of the Chesapeake and the rich and fertile country adjoining, afforded great

facility and additional inducement for the enemy to push their operations in that quarter, and the events of that crisis show, from the great deficiency in our military establishment, especially in the Department of Military Supplies, that it was for a length of time before the progress of the enemy could be checked or arrested ; and independent of the causes which have existed, it is believed that in a similar encounter the enemy would renew his design, and as military positions are chosen for general and particular purposes in relation to definite objects, it was found that Baltimore became the natural point for the concentration of the military forces for ulterior operations, and it was determined by the Government to erect an arsenal and depot somewhere in the rear of that city, to afford the facility of supplies to the forces operating in the immediate vicinity, as well as those permanent military posts constructed for the defense of this section of our maritime frontier. In the selection of the site for this establishment, two things presented themselves,--the topography of the country, and the means that an enemy might have in operating upon it, and it is believed that on a proper view of the country adjacent to Baltimore, the site for this depot was as judiciously chosen as the nature of the case would admit of; Secondly, it will be seen from the extent of these works (the drawings of which accompany this report,) that they combine in themselves the advantage of an arsenal of construction, as well as a depot of military supplies, and can usefully employ one or two companies of citizens, as the nature of the service may require.

"This arsenal is situated on the Reisterstown turnpike road, eight miles from the City of Baltimore. This road is smooth and firm at all seasons of the year, and affords the best land transportation; it extends back north and northwest of the arsenal and passes through the upper counties of Maryland and into the productive counties of Pennsylvania, and is a great land thoroughfare to Baltimore, thereby presenting to the establishment the advantage of procuring land transportation in time of war with ease and on advantageous terms. The general aspect of the country around the arsenal is remarkable for its fertility of soil, gently rolling and well wooded, and is watered by Jones' and Gwynn's Falls, whose headwaters take their rise in the vicinity of the post and present on both sides a number of springs of pure water. The situation is very healthy, the whole country around is remarkable for its salubrious air, and but few local diseases prevail ; these advantages render it a proper position for an encampment of troops and of military supplies. The means by which stores are transported from this arsenal to the permanent posts intended to be supplied from it, are by hauling them to Baltimore, or to the head of the navigable waters of the Severn River and from thence by water. The navigation of the Patapsco is obstructed by ice a part of the months of December and January, but no longer than from twenty to thirty days ; unless the season is unusually cold, it is kept open for commercial advantages. The navigation of the Severn is not usually obstructed by ice, hence this route can be resorted to in case the first fails, and in the event of both these routes being obstructed by the ice, the posts for the interior defense can be supplied by land transportation at short notice, and the fortifications for exterior defense can be readily sup-

plied by taking the stores to Annapolis, where the navigation is scarcely
ever known to be closed by ice, and from thence shipped. The distance
of this arsenal from Baltimore is eight miles; to Fort McHenry, eleven
miles; to the head of the navigable waters of the Severn River, eighteen
to twenty miles, and to Fort Severn and Annapolis, thirty-five miles.
The roads are firm and passable at all seasons of the year. The posts on
the interior line of defense can be supplied with stores at all times; the
nearest to the arsenal, three and a half or four hours; the most remote,
from about eighteen to twenty-four hours. The fortifications on the exterior line of defense can be supplied at all seasons of the year within
from thirty-six to forty-eight hours. Annexed is a sketch showing the
relative position of the arsenal to the principal cities, towns and water
courses in the vicinity, and also the roads to and from the arsenal."

[Signed.]   N. BADEN,
1st Lieutenant on Ordnance duty.

Shortly after, or during the late war, the arsenal was abandoned as a
military post, and in 1880, the Federal Government relinquished the same
to the state of Maryland. The commandant in 1860, just preceding the
commencement of the war, was that distinguished soldier, Major, afterwards Lieut.-General Huger. The State, after taking possession of the
property, made no practical use of it; in fact, it was an item of expense
for several years, by reason of the salary of a custodian. No repairs had
been placed on the property for a period of some twenty years, and the
condition at the time of the transfer to the care of the Maryland Line
was little short of that of a ruin. Work was at once commenced to rescue
it from this sad plight in April, 1888, and on June 27th, in the same year,
had so far progressed as to admit of the formal opening and dedication.
Appropriate exercises were held, with a large attendance of citizens from
Baltimore and the neighboring country. Addresses were made by Hon.
Geo. Wm. Brown, who presided, Gen. A. H. Colquitt, U. S. Senator from
Georgia; Gen. Chas. E. Hooker, member of Congress from Mississippi;
Hon. Ferd. C. Latrobe, Mayor of Baltimore City; Hon. C. Ridgely Goodwin, State Senator from Baltimore City; Gen. Bradley T. Johnson, and
others. Every year since, reunions and like celebrations have taken place,
which have been frequently graced by the attendance of distinguished
Confederates, many of whom have, since the war, been prominent in the
national councils of the country.

The administration of the home rests with the Board of Governors of
the Association of the Maryland Line, and is under the immediate supervision of a Board of Managers, who are largely aided in their duties by
the labors of a Board of Visitors, which is made up of well known ladies,
who give the benefit of their counsel and are untiring in their efforts in
caring for the sick and ministering to their wants. The command of the
Home is intrusted to a superintendent, Mr. W. H. Pope, a gallant soldier
of the Maryland Line, who, with his devoted wife, have faithfully given
their entire services to the institution.

It was determined from the first to make the institution in fact what
it was in name—a home for those who sought its sheltering care, and
this view was held in the furnishing of the rooms, and the rules enacted for

the government of the inmates. These last have been framed so as to insure the least restraint possible with the maintenance of proper discipline and decorum. The separate buildings have been named after distinguished Maryland Confederate-soldiers or sailors, and the rooms have been furnished as memorials by the friends or relations of some loved one who gave his life for the cause, or who was conspicuous for his gallantry or devotion. These rooms have been furnished in a substantial manner, with many of the comforts and elegancies found in private homes, and at an estimated cost of ten thousand dollars, which expense has been defrayed by the generous friends undertaking this important and interesting feature. As a result, the management have been relieved almost entirely of the great expense incident to the furnishing of the Home, and their means made available for the necessary repairs of the property and the purchase of proper equipment and supplies required by an institution of this character.

The State has continued to make appropriation, which, supplemented by generous private contributions, both in money and material, have enabled the management to maintain the high standard of comfort originally had in view, and at the same time there has been due regard to proper economy.

The total admissions, from the opening in June, 1888, to December 1st, 1893, a period of nearly five and a half years, have been 139. Of this number 27 have died, three have been suspended or otherwise discharged; the number now borne on the roster is 109.

The medical administration is in the hands of the surgeon, Dr. W. P. E. Wyse, who daily visits the Home and is most attentive to the wants of the inmates.

The library is supplied with many valuable and interesting books and periodicals, the gift of friends, and the newspapers of the States regularly mail their issues without charge.

The total receipts of the Home to September 30th, 1893, were $37,-620.40, and the expenses $38,195.00, leaving a deficit as of the above date, $574.60. Of the receipts, the State of Maryland has contributed $27,500.00, and the remainder is the result of private subscriptions and the proceeds of entertainments, held at various times in the interest of the Home. Included in the item of expenses is the sum of $8,118.42, the cost of repairs to the property.

Attention is invited to the description of the Home and other interesting statements, which will be found in this publication, and a cordial invitation is extended to the public to visit the institution.

Here will be found a noble charity, creditable to the honor of our State and the public spirit of our citizens. It is a comfort to the old veterans, who feel that if adversity proves too strong for them in their declining years, a haven of rest is here provided, to which they may retire and find refuge, and, at the same time, lose none of their self-respect, nor suffer in the estimation of those whose experience in life is more fortunate; and it is a standing illustration to the young that our loved Commonwealth reveres manliness and courage, and is proud of the military record of the past and is not unmindful of its heroes in their old age.

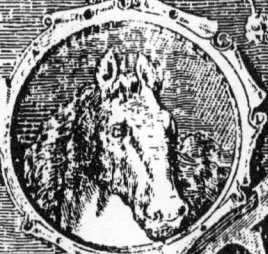

BOARD OF GOVERNORS AND MANAGERS.

No. 1. WM. H. FITZGERALD, *Treasurer*.   No. 5. JOHN F. HAYDEN,
"   2. CAPT. GEO. W. BOOTH, *Secretary*,   "   6. JAMES L. AUBREY,
"   3.   "   A. C. TRIPPE,   "   7. DR. W. P. E. WYSE, *Surgeon*.
"   4. WM. H. POPE, *Superintendent*,   "   8. CAPT. JOHN W. TORSCH.

INTERIOR VIEW OF COURTYARD.

DESCRIPTION OF MEMORIAL

And other rooms in the respective Buildings.

1.—TRIMBLE BUILDING,   6.—SEMMES BUILDING,

2.—BUCHANAN "   7.—ELZEY "

3.—LITTLE "   8.—WINDER "

4.—TILGHMAN "   9.—MACKALL "

5.—ARCHER "   10.—JACKSON "

THE MAJOR GENL. ISAAC R. TRIMBLE BUILDING

Contains the Relic Hall, also a Bath Room and the following Memorial Rooms: Capt. R. B. Buck, Frank H. Sanderson, First Maryland Artillery, Zollinger and Col. Harry Gilmor.

Genl. Trimble was born May 15th, 1802. Cadet at West Point, 1818; Graduated 1822; resigned 1832; entered the Confederate service May 1861, and appointed Colonel of Engineers; and September 3rd, 1861 ordered to command of river batteries at Evansport; November 13th, 1861 relieved from duty at Evansport and assigned November 16th, 1861 to command of Third Brigade, Second Division, Army of Northern Virginia; November 22nd, 1861, assigned to command of Fourth Brigade, Second Division, Army of Northern Virginia; October 26th, 1862, recommended by Genl. Lee to be promoted to Major General to command Jackson's Division; January 19th, 1863, promoted to Major General; May 28th, 1863, assigned to command of Shenandoah Valley; engaged at Cold Harbor, Gaines' Mill, Malvern Hill, Westover, Winchester (1863), Port Republic, Cross Keys, Slaughter Mountain, Cedar Run, Hazel River and capture of Manassas Junction, August 26th, 1862, and Gettysburg. At Cross Keys, Genl. Ewell in his report says, "Trimble's Brigade had the brunt of action and is entitled to most thanks." August 26th, 1862, Gen. Trimble, with a force of 500 men, was voluntarily detached from Jackson's Army, and, in co-operation with a portion of Stuart's Cavalry, captured a vast quantity of Quartermaster's commissary and ordnance stores at Manassas Junction, which was then far in the rear of the Federal Army. His loss was but fifteen men wounded, and the capture amounted to eight guns and three hundred prisoners, besides the immense stores. General Trimble was twice severely wounded, once at the second battle of Manassas, and at Gettysburg, where he was taken prisoner. At Gettysburg he commanded Major Genl. Pender's Division.

MEMORIAL ROOM TO CAPT. RICHARD B. BUCK.

This room is furnished in oak with four beds, dressing case, wardrobes, tables, rockers, woven wire springs, and hair mattresses for the beds. A beautiful china toilet set, a rich drugget and rugs, also lace curtains at the windows; furnished by Mrs. R. B. Buck.

MEMORIAL ROOM TO FRANK H. SANDERSON.

In this room a fine picture of this brave and handsome youth hangs on the wall, and underneath is a tablet, which reads thus:

IN MEMORIAM.

On the 4th day of July, 1863 after receiving a fatal wound the day previous, at that ever memorable battle of Gettysburg, Frank H. Sanderson yielded up his young life in the cause he loved so well. He enlisted in Capt. Wm. H. Murray's Co. A, 2nd Maryland Infantry, August 26th, 1862. In September of the same year his command was ordered to Winchester, and under the command of Genl. W. E. Jones, experienced a great deal of very hard service, in all of which Frank H. Sanderson was an active participant. Furnished by his brother, W. Cook Sanderson, of Baltimore City.

FIRST MARYLAND ARTILLERY ROOM.

This was one of the best known and most efficient Artillery organizations in the Army of Northern Virginia. The room has been furnished through the liberality of Lieut. Col. R. Snowden Andrews, who was the first Captain, and who was succeeded by that gallant soldier, Capt. Wm. F. Dement. Capt. Andrews was distinguished for his skill and soldierly conduct and bearing. He was promoted to the rank of Lieut. Colonel of Artillery and was severely wounded at Mechanicsville, Cedar Mountain and Jordan Springs.

ZOLLINGER MEMORIAL ROOM

In memory of Lieut. Wm. P. Zollinger and his brother Jacob E. Zollinger. This room is furnished very handsomely and its wants are always kept supplied. Wm. P. Zollinger enlisted in the Confederate Service, Co. H, 1st Maryland Infantry, June 18th, 1861; discharged August 1862. Again enlisted in Co. A, 2nd Maryland Infantry, August 20th, 1862, and elected 2nd Lieutenant; was wounded on the Weldon R. R., also at Pegram's Farm. Jacob E. Zollinger enlisted August 20th, 1862, in Co. A, 2nd Maryland Infantry; was severely wounded at Gettysburg, July 1863, from effects of which he eventually died. This room is furnished by Mrs. Chas. A. Oakford, Mrs. Wm. P. Zollinger, and Mrs. W. G. Power.

LIEUTENANT COLONEL HARRY GILMOR ROOM.

This room was furnished by the survivors of his old command, and is one of the handsomest in the home. Col. Gilmor enlisted in the Confederate Service August 31st, 1861, as a private in Capt. Frank Mason's Co. G, Ashby's Regiment of Cavalry; March 27th, 1862, was elected Captain; May 7th, 1863, was commissioned Major and subsequently Lieutenant Colonel in command 2nd Maryland Cavalry.

ARTICLES TO BE FOUND IN THE RELIC HALL.

1. Fac-simile of the engrossed Constitution of the Confederate States of America, and signatures thereto.
2. Uniform jacket, pants, hat, &c., of Wm. H. Pope, Co. D, 1st Maryland Cavalry, worn during the War 1861–1865.

3. Officer's Coat worn by Lieut. H. H. Bean, Co. I, 1st Md. Inft.
4. Confederate Soldier's Haversack.
5. Confederate Battle Flag.
6. John Brown—Pike captured during the John Brown raid at Harper's Ferry, W. Va., October 16th, 1859.
7. Regimental Colors of the 2nd Maryland Infantry, C. S. A., carried by them at Gettysburg, being the first flag planted on Culp's Hill in the works captured by Steuart's Brigade, July 2nd, 1863.
8. Colors presented to the Frederick Volunteers, Co. A, 1st Maryland Infantry, and carried by the 1st Maryland Infantry in the first Battle of Manassas and other engagements.
9. Headquarter Flag used by Genl. Bradley T. Johnson at Headquarters of the Maryland Line, 1861-65.
10. Battle Flag of the 1st Maryland Cavalry, 1861-65.
11. Confederate Battle Flag presented by Mrs. Fannie A. Beers.
12. Drum used by Hosea Pitt, Drum Major, 1st Maryland Infantry, 1861-65.
13. Confederate Candle or Taper used in the C. S. A.
14. Confederate Field Glass found on the Battlefield of Gettysburg.
15. Walking Cane cut from a tree which grew over Stonewall Jackson's Grave.
16. Uniform Coat belonging to and worn by Admiral Franklin Buchanan in the engagement between the Virginia and Monitor at Hampton Roads and at Mobile Bay.
17. Home-made Splint used by Admiral Buchanan for wound received in Mobile Bay.
18. Bullet cut from a tree at Cold Harbor, Va.
19. C. S. A. Belt Buckle.
20. Sabre worn by W. H. Pope during the war.
21. Piece of Corner Stone of Gen. R. E. Lee's Monument at Richmond, Va.
22. Shell found on the Battlefield of Gettysburg, by Hugh McWilliams, July 25th, 1866.
23. Seal of the Confederates States of America.
24. Photograph of Genl. A. P. Hill.
25. Pistol and holster used by W. H. Pope, Co. D, 1st Maryland Cavalry, C. S. A.
26. Coupon cut from a Confederate Bond.
27. Three Flints issued to Corporal E. H. Browne, Co. C, 16th Virginia Infantry, about April 25th, 1861.
28. Coat worn by Admiral Buchanan, 1861—65.
26. Original Muster Roll of Capt. Ed. R. Dorsey's Co., 1st Maryland Infantry, C. S. A.
30. C. S. A. State Paper, from Judah P. Benjamin.
31. Fork used by E. H. Browne in the Officers' Mess, C. S. Gun Boat, Chicamauga.
32. Stars and Bars.
33. Picture of Confederate Officers in their old United States uniform.
34. Five orders (framed) issued by Genl. Isaac R. Trimble in Baltimore City, April and May 1861.

35. Pictures—Stonewall Jackson at the Battle of Chancellorsville.
36. Confederate Steamer Alabama, or 290, and officers.
37. Admiral Franklin Buchanan.
38. Members of the Maryland Line Confederate Soldiers' Home and their friends at Pen Mar, September 19th, 1890.
39. Admiral Raphael Semmes.
40. Brig. Genl. Henry Little.
41. Major General Isaac R. Trimble.
42. In Memoriam.
43. Brig. General George H. Steuart. Genl. Steuart is a graduate of West Point; he resigned his commission as Captain of Cavalry at commencement of the war, and was made Lieut. Col. 1st Maryland Infantry; promoted to Colonel July 21st, 1861, and to Brigadier General March 18th, 1862. He was a gallant and efficient officer and is at present a resident of Anne Arundel County, Maryland. He is the senior Confederate Officer from Maryland now living.
44. General Lloyd Tilghman.
45. Commodore Geo. N. Hollins. Commodore Hollins was born in Baltimore, Md., September 20th, 1799, entered the U. S. Navy as Midshipman in 1814, became a Lieutenant in the Navy 1825, and a Commander in 1841; promoted to a Captaincy in 1855. He resigned in 1861, joined the Confederate Service and was commissioned as Commodore. He with Zarvona Thomas captured the Steamer St. Nicholas, on the Potomac River, June 29th, 1861; placed in charge of the Naval defenses of James River. Commodore Hollins, in September 1861, was placed in charge of the Fleet on the Mississippi River and at the New Orleans Naval Station, July 1861.
46. General Charles S. Winder.
47. Lieutenant Colonel Harry Gilmor.
48. General T. J. Jackson. (Stonewall.)
49. General Joseph E. Johnston.
50. Confederate Memorial Tablet.
51. General Robert E. Lee.
52. Stonewall Jackson.
53. Farewell address of Major General T. T. Mumford, to the 1st Maryland Cavalry, April 25th, 1865.
54. General Robert E. Lee and Staff.
55. General A. P. Hill.
56. Governor Wade Hampton.
57. Hugh McWilliams, Company C. 1st Maryland Cavalry.
58. Burial of Latane.
59. F. Nichols Crouch, author of "Kathleen Mavoureen."
60. Soldier Quaker Guns.
61. Memorial Picture, Confederate Officers.
62. Jefferson Davis.
63. Appomattox.
64. Battle Flag, Confederate.
65. Lee at Stonewall Jackson's grave.

66. General Robert E. Lee.
67. Confederate Flags.
68. Views at the Home.
69. Views at the Home.
70. Lieut. Col. Ridgely Brown.
71. General Hood's Family.
72. Brig. Genl. James J. Archer, Harford County, Md.
73. Lieut. Col. James R. Herbert. Colonel Herbert was born August 18th, 1833; Captain Co D, 1st Maryland Infantry, C. S. A. 1861-62; Lieutenant Colonel commanding 2nd Maryland Infantry, C. S. A. 1862-65.
74. Mosby and his men.
75. Brig. General Bradley T. Johnson.
76. Major General Arnold Elzey.
77. Brig. General Bradley T. Johnson, taken during the war.
78. President Jefferson Davis and his Cabinet.

RELICS.

79. Two Confederate Notes ($100.00 and $50.00) which were in the pocket book of General Robert E. Lee, at the surrender.
80. Two Ambrotypes and Letter brought from the Seven days Battlefield around Richmond, Va., by Wm. H. Pope, Co. A, 1st Maryland Infantry.
81. Bullet dug from the Breastworks of Fort Hell on the Plank Road near Petersburg, Va., by John Walsh, 1104 Mosher St., Baltimore.
82. Discharge and parole of L. H. Schoolfield, Baltimore Light Artillery.

ADMIRAL FRANKLIN BUCHANAN BUILDING.

This building, in memory of the above distinguished Naval Commander, contains four memorial rooms, Jenkins, Gill, Brown and Murray.

Franklin Buchanan was born in Baltimore, Md., September 11th, 1800; he entered the United States Naval January 28th, 1815, became Lieutenant January 13th, 1825, Master Commander September 8th, 1841, First Superintendent of the Annapolis Naval Academy 1845, Captain September 14th, 1855; 1861 in charge of the Naval Yard at Washington; resigned his commission, and on the 5th of September 1861 entered the Confederate Service and was assigned to duty as Chief of Orders and Details; ordered to the command of the Virginia (old Merrimac) February 24th, 1862; March 1862 Flag Officer of the James River Squadron; March 8th, 1862 in the battle between the Virginia and Monitor, and seriously wounded; Admiral, August 21st, 1862; June 1863 assigned to the Naval Force at Mobile, on the Flag Ship, Baltic; wounded in the leg at Mobile Bay and taken prisoner August 1864.

JENKINS ROOM.

This room was furnished by Geo. C. Jenkins, Esq., in memory of his brother, John Carrell Jenkins, who lost his life October 11th, 1861, in his Country's Cause. This room is in oak, very tastefully furnished with everything comfortable. It contains a very quaint old chimney and fireplace.

ESTABLISHED IN 1816.

THE CHAS. SIMON'S SONS CO.

FOREIGN, AND DOMESTIC

Dry Goods,

NO. 208 NORTH HOWARD ST.,

BALTIMORE, MD.

J. W. BREEDLOVE,

Men's and Youth's

Merchant Tailor,

Fine Domestic Suitings, ... $20.

Imported London Shrunk Suitings, $25.

J. W. BREEDLOVE,   **4 ST. PAUL ST.,**   Near Baltimore — Street. —

Fifteen years in charge of Custom Department of NOAH WALKER & CO.

BOARD OF GOVERNORS AND MANAGERS.

No. 1. JAS. R. WHEELER, *Chairman.*   No. 5. AUGUST SIMON,
" 2. COL. GEO. R. GAITHER,   " 6. CHAS. KETTLEWELL,
" 3. R. J. STINSON,   " 7. DAN'L L. THOMAS,
" 4. MARK O. SHRIVER,   " 8. CAPT. CHAS. H. CLAIBORNE.

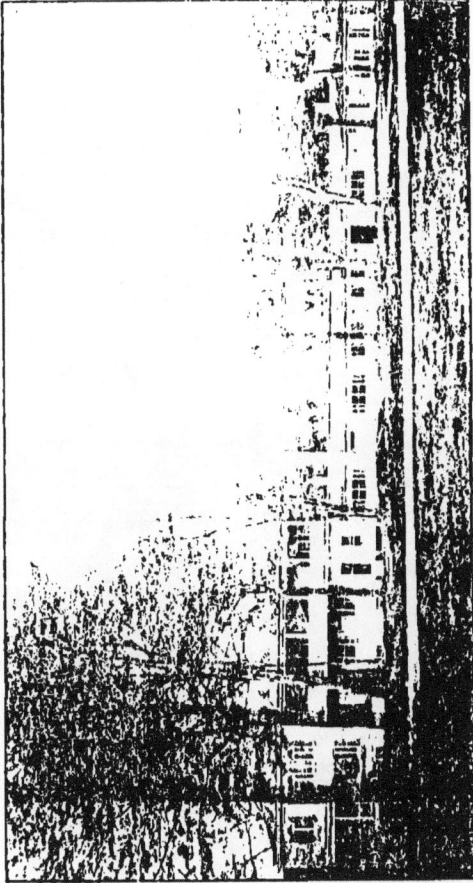

INTERIOR VIEW OF COURTYARD.

J. C. Jenkins was a member of Maryland Guards, which company was in the 21st Virginia Infantry. Geo. C. Jenkins, who furnished this room also served the cause faithfully in Company C, Maryland Cavalry.

GILL ROOM.

Furnished by Mr. John Gill, in memory of his brother, Sommerville P. Gill, who was killed at Pegram's Farm, Va. He was a member of Co. A, 2nd Maryland Infantry.

This room is furnished in cherry ; contains 4 beds, wire springs, hair mattresses, wardrobe, dressing case, stove, lamp and table. The floor is covered with a large rug, rocking chairs, and all that goes to make a room comfortable.

Mr. John Gill was also a Confederate Soldier ; he served in Co. H, 1st Maryland Infantry, and afterwards in the Signal Corps of the Army of Northern Virginia.

RIDGELY BROWN ROOM.

Was furnished through the efforts of Mrs. John F. Hunter, by subscriptions of money and donations of articles suitable. This room contains 4 beds, wire springs ; hair mattresses, dressing case, wardrobes, and everything to add to the comfort of its occupants. The room is in the memory of the gallant Lieut. Col. Ridgely Brown, of Montgomery County, Md. who lost his life on the South Anna, Va., June 1st, 1864, on the field of battle. He was Lieutenant Colonel of the 1st Maryland Cavalry, and was one of Maryland's best and bravest soldiers, his picture adorns the wall of this room, also a copy of the General Order published at the time of his death, which reads as follows :

"HEADQUARTERS, MARYLAND LINE, JUNE 26TH, 1864.

General Order, No. 26.

Lieut. Col. Ridgely Brown, Commanding the 1st Maryland Cavalry, fell in battle on the 1st instant, near the South Anna. He died as a soldier prefers to die, leading his men in a victorious charge. As an officer, kind and careful,—as a soldier, brave and true—as a gentleman, chivalrous—as a christian, gentle and modest. No one in the Confederate Army surpassed him in the hold he had upon the hearts of his men and the place in the esteem of his superiors ; of the rich blood Maryland has lavished on every battle-field, none is more precious than this, and that of our other brave comrades in arms who fell during the four days previous in the hill-sides of Hanover. His command has lost a friend most steadfast, but his commanding officer is deprived of an assistant invaluable. To the first he was ever careful, as a father ; to the latter, as true as a brother. In token of respect to his memory, the colors of the different regiments of this command will be draped, and the officers wear the usual badge of mourning for thirty days.

By order of, COL. BRADLEY T. JOHNSON,
GEO. W. BOOTH, A. A. G."

Col. Brown went to Virginia on the 1st of June, 1861 ; was Lieutenant in Co. K, 1st Virginia Cavalry, afterwards in 1862 made Captain Co. A, 1st Maryland Cavalry, which was the nucleus of that organization and to which he was promoted Major and subsequently Lieutenant Colonel commanding.

MURRAY ROOM.

This room is furnished by the Murray Association in memory of their Captain, Wm. H. Murray, of Anne Arundel County, Md. He entered the service of the Confederate States June 18th, 1861, and was killed at Gettysburg July 1863. His picture hangs on the wall ; also a picture of his monument at Loudon Park Cemetery. This room is in oak and contains 4 beds with woven wire springs and hair mattresses. The floor is covered with a large rug, and the other furniture consists of wardrobes, washstand, dressing case, tables, toilet set and various other articles which enure to the comfort of the members.

Capt. Murray was a most lovable character, modest and unassuming in disposition, pure and chaste in his conversation, tender and considerate for those under his charge ; no one occupied a warmer place in the affections of their men than did this gallant soldier. His soldierly qualities were as marked as was his personal character unblemished. He will ever live in the memory of those who knew him, and their sorrow over his early fall is just as keen to.day as it was thirty years ago. To their children will his character be handed down as an example worthy of emulation, as a Maryland soldier who reflected the honor of his State and whose private life was bright with christian virtues.

BRIGADIER GENERAL. HENRY LITTLE BUILDING.

This building contains a bath room and memorial rooms as follows : Virginia, McKim, Baltimore Light Artillery, Little, Colston, Marshall, Stonebraker, Goodwin, and Chantilly.

Gen. Little was born in Baltimore, March 19th, 1817 ; his record is as follows : U. S. Army, 2nd Lieutenant 5th Infantry, July 1st, 1839 ; 1st Lieutenant 7th Infantry, April 18th, 1845 ; Brevet Captain for gallant conduct at Monterey, Mexico, September 23rd, 1846 ; Captain 7th Infantry August 20th, 1847 ; resigned May 7th, 1861.

Confederate States Army : Colonel and Adjutant General, Staff of Gen. Price, May 1861 ; Brigadier General April 16th, 1862 ; April 22nd, 1862, Brigadier General in Command of Confederate forces in the vicinity of Rienza, on the Mobile and Ohio Railroad.

Gen. Henry Little was engaged in the battles of Pea Ridge, or Elkhorn Tavern, Arkansas, March 6th—8th, 1862 ; killed at battle of Iuka, Miss. September 19th, 1862, commanding 1st Division, Army of the West.

In a letter from Genl. Earl Van Dorn to Genl. Beauregard, dated April 27th, 1862, he says : "I want Little as Major General."

General Van Dorn, in his report of the battle of Pea Ridge, or Elkhorn Tavern, says : "To Col. Henry Little my especial thanks are due for the coolness, skill and devotion with which for two days he and his gallant brigade bore the brunt of the battle."

Genl. S. Price, in his report of the same battle, says: "The brunt of the action fell during the early part of the day upon my right wing, consisting of Genl. Slack's and Col. Little's brigades; they pushed forward gallantly against heavy odds, and the most stubborn resistance, and were victorious everywhere."

Gen. S. Price, in his report of his retreat from Missouri, says: "Col. Henry Little commanding the 1st Brigade * * * covered the retreat from beyond Cassville and acted as the rear guard. The Colonel commanding deserves the highest praise for increasing watchfulness and the good management of his entire command. I heartily commend him to your attention."

Genl. Sterling Price, in his report of the battle of Iuka, says: "It will thus be seen that our success was obtained at the sacrifice of many a brave officer and patriot soldier, chief among them was Brig. Genl. Little, commanding the 1st Division of this Army. Than this brave Marylander no one could have fallen more dear to me, or whose memory should be more fondly cherished by his countrymen. Than him, no more skillful officer, or more devout patriot has drawn his sword in this War of Independence. He died in the day of his greatest usefulness, lamented by his friends, by the brigade of his love, by the Division which he so ably commanded and by the Army of the West, of which he had from the beginning been one of the chief ornaments."

Brig. Genl. Louis Herbert, in his report of the same battle, says: "Early in the action, when the main charge had been ordered, Brigadier General Little was instantly killed by a minnie ball, and the command of the Division devolved on the undersigned. The fall of the General was immediately known throughout the lines, but far from creating consternation, panic or confusion, every officer and every soldier seemed to become animated with new determination. The leader whom they had learned to love and esteem, and in whom they had full confidence, had fallen—the foe who had deprived them of him was in front, and revenge was within their grasp. The 1st Division of the Army of the West will ever remember and venerate the name of Henry Little."

VIRGINIA ROOM.

The Virginia Room was furnished through the efforts of Mrs. Martin B. Brown, by subscriptions, in honor of old Virginia. This is a beautiful room, contains 2 beds and is furnished in walnut. The appointments are of the first class, the toilet china is inscribed with the name "Virginia" in gilt.

McKIM ROOM.

Furnished by Mrs. William Reed, in memory of her brother, Robert B. McKim, who was a member of the Rockbridge Artillery. He entered the Confederate Service April 20th, 1861; was engaged in the battles of Manassas, Kernstown and Winchester, where he was killed May 25, 1862, aged 18 years. The furniture of this room is in oak, with two beds, and is very tastefully furnished.

THE BALTIMORE LIGHT ARTILLERY ROOM.

This room is most tastefully and comfortably furnished by the surviving members of that battery, the 2nd Maryland Artillery, in memory of their deceased comrades.

The Baltimore Light Artillery was one of the best known batteries in the Artillery arm of the Confederate Service, and no one organization did more to maintain the honor of our State and her fair fame, than did this body of young Marylanders. The Battery was formed in the early part of the fall of 1861, and was ordered to report to Genl. J. E. Johnston, then in command of the Army at Centreville, Va. The intelligence of its commanders—the gallantry and skill with which their guns were handled, soon attracted the attention of all, and from the actions in the Valley, under Jackson, the severe battles around Richmond, to the culmination of their active operations in 1862 at Sharpsburg, their valor and devotion were most conspicuous. After the return to Virginia, the battery was directed to report to Genl. W. E. Jones, in command of the Valley District, who had also under his command the 1st Maryland Cavalry and the 2nd Maryland Infantry. From this time on, the battery served with the Cavalry Corps. In this service they added to the high reputation they had already achieved, and no service was too arduous for them to undertake—no danger too great for them to face, and in no instance did they ever prove unworthy of the confidence which was reposed in them by those in whose support they were so frequently called upon to take positions of greatest peril. Under the gallant Brockenborough, Griffin and McNulty, they achieved a fame second to no similar organization, and its surviving members have been as true to each other in the latter days of peace, as were they in the trying scenes which proved their manhood and courage. They have maintained the memories of the past by forming a social organization, and the furnishing of this memorial room is but one of the fruits of their love and appreciation of the cause for which they so nobly fought, endured privation, and for which so many of their number died.

GENERAL HENRY LITTLE ROOM.

Furnished by Mrs. Henry Little in memory of her husband. This room is handsomely furnished with oak furniture ; contains 2 beds woven wire springs and hair mattresses. The pillows in this room were made of the feathers from the game which Genl. Little shot during his life time. A fine picture of the General also adorns the wall of the room ; also portraits of Lee and Jackson, the charge of the First Maryland Infantry, the prayer in Stonewall Jackson's Camp.

MARSHALL ROOM.

In memory of Brothers Robert I. Taylor Marshall, a member of the Washington Artillery ; killed at Beverly's Ford, August 23rd, 1862 ; and James Markam Marshall, of the Black Horse Company, of the Fourth Virginia Cavalry, who died for his country September 5th, 1862.

The room contains oak furniture, and was furnished by their brother Col. Charles Marshall, of Genl. Robert E. Lee's Staff.

STONEBRAKER ROOM.

This room is substantially furnished by Joseph R. Stonebraker, who was a member of Company C, First Maryland Cavalry, as a memorial to his brother, Edward L. Stonebraker.

GOODWIN ROOM.

Furnished by C. Ridgely Goodwin, Esq., in memory of his brother, Frank Greenwood Goodwin. This room is furnished in oak and is very comfortable.

Frank Greenwood Goodwin, tenth child of Robert Morris Goodwin, of Maryland, was born in Savannah, Ga., November 13th, 1846. He was at school at Chattanooga, Tenn., early in 1861. In April 1861 he joined the Oglethorpe Light Infantry, of Savannah, and with that company went to Virginia, under command of Capt. Frank Bartow, taking part in the first Battle of Manassas (Bull Run). The Company became a part of the 8th Georgia Regiment, G. T. Andrews' Brigade, Hood's Division, Longstreet's Corps. At the Battle of Seven Pines he was shot through the arm, went to his home, and within a month returned to his command. Participating in all the battles of the Army of Northern Virginia, Frank Goodwin gave his life to his country at Gettysburg, July 3, 1863, aged 17.

If there is anything in the theory of heredity, Frank Goodwin could not help from being a rebel; his ancestors were rebels in the time of Moses—his ancestors were rebels at the Battle of Sterling, under William Wallace—his ancestors were rebels under Cromwell—his Grandfather was an officer under the rebel, George Washington—his Father was an officer under Andrew Jackson, at New Orleans, and it was in the natural order of things that this boy and his brothers should be rebels under Robert E. Lee. "That which is bred in the bone, must come out in the flesh."

CHANTILLY ROOM.

This is a small hall room, with a single bed, and furnished by Mrs. H. F. Going, who has been active and helpful in all matters connected with Confederate Work.

Chantilly was an estate on the picket line, while the Army was encamped at Centreville, in the Autumn of 1861, and is associated with pleasant recollections by members of the First Maryland Infantry.

WILLIAM E. COLSTON ROOM.

This room was one of the first furnished and presents an attractive and comfortable appearance.

William E. Colston was born in Washington, March 24th, 1839, but his early years were spent in Virginia, the home of his ancestors. He came to Baltimore about 1857, and was among the first to go to Virginia when the war broke out.

On June 1st, 1861, he enlisted as a private in Co. B, Maryland Guard, attached to the 21st Virginia Infantry, but when the 1st Maryland Regiment was formed, was transferred to Co. H, Capt. Wm. H. Murray, June 18th, 1861. In this Company he served in all the campaigns and battles of the year, and at the Battle of Cross Keys, June 8th, 1862, in

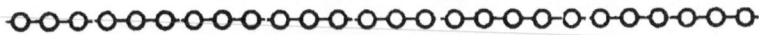

COMMANDANT'S HOUSE.

STONEWALL JACKSON INFIRMARY AND OLD POWDER MAGAZINE.

Jackson's Valley Campaign, he was desperately wounded, being shot through the body. He was permanently injured by this wound and disabled for a long time, but as soon as able to ride, he was appointed Volunteer Aid to Major General Trimble. General Trimble being wounded and left at Gettysburg, Colston then volunteered into Mosby's command, and was killed in the night attack on Harper's Ferry, January 10th, 1864. He is buried in the Confederate lot at London Park with his old comrades of Co. H.

The room was furnished by his brother, Capt. Frederick M. Colston, Assistant to Chief Ordnance Officer, Army Northern Virginia.

BRIG. GENL. LLOYD TILGHMAN BUILDING.

Genl. Lloyd Tilghman of Talbot Co., Md., was educated at West Point. At Fort Henry, February 6th, 1862, he held the Fort until nearly half his gunners were killed or wounded. When Foote took the Fort he had as prisoners Genl. Tilghman and Staff, and sixty men. Genl. Tilghman remained as prisoner a few months and was exchanged. In the fall of 1862 he rejoined the Army of the West, then in Mississippi, and was put in command of the First Brigade, Loring's Division. At the Battle of Corinth he took a prominent part, and in all subsequent operations of that Army, under Van Dorn, and afterwards Pemberton, he bore a conspicuous part up to the time of his death. Genl. Tilghman was killed by a shell on the evening of the 16th of May, 1863, on the battlefield of Baker's Creek or Champion Hill, Mississippi.

This building contains temporarily the carpenter shop and paint shops. It is proposed to remove these shops and thus render space available for the fitting up of two rooms. This will be done as soon as the circumstances of the Home will admit. An opportunity is here presented to furnish two additional memorial rooms. 2627396

BRIG. GENERAL JAMES J. ARCHER BUILDING.

Genl. James J. Archer was born in Harford County, Md.; Colonel of the 5th Texas Regiment, commanding Texas Brigade at Evansport Batteries, March 21st, 1862. Acting Brig. Genl. at West Point, Va., May 7th, 1862; promoted to Brig. Genl. June 2d, 1862, and assigned command of 5th Brigade, Hill's Division. June 4th, 1862, assigned to Hatton's Brigade, Whiting's Division ; June 26th and 28th, 1862, engaged in the Battles of Mechanicsville and Gaines' Mill ; August 9th, 1862, in Battle of Cedar Mountain ; August 26th, 1862, engagement at Manassas Junction ; August 28th, 29th and 30th, 1862, Second Manassas ; September 1st, 1862, Ox Hill ; September 15th, 1862, at Harper's Ferry ; September 17th, 1862, Sharpsburg ; September 20th, 1862, Shepherdstown ; December 11th-15th, 1862, Fredericksburg ; May 3d, 1863, Chancellorsville ; July 1st, 1863, Gettysburg, where he was wounded and captured.

Genl. Early in his report said. "The service lost at this time that most gallant and meritorious officer, Brig. Genl. Archer, who fell into the enemy's hands ;" His death resulted from his wounds and his imprisonment on Morris Island, South Carolina, where 800 officers were imprisoned in the line of the fire from the Confederate batteries and forts.

This Building contains on the lower floor the Raleigh C. Thomas Memorial Hall ; on the second floor a store room and servants' sleeping quarters.

RALEIGH C. THOMAS HALL..

The Thomas Memorial Hall was furnished by the family and friends of Raleigh C. Thomas, who was a gallant soldier in Co. C, 1st Maryland Cavalry, and who was much beloved by his comrades. This room, which is 50x27 feet, is used as a Reading Room. It is furnished in old oak with most comfortable and handsome furniture, tables, arm chairs and rockers. The ceiling is of oak, and the equipping of the room involved an expense of about $1000.00. It is a handsome tribute to the memory of the deceased, who died in Baltimore in 1887. A fine painting of Mr. Thomas is on the wall. The Library contains 1000 volumes contributed at various times by kind friends from all over the State, about 100 newspapers are on file, which are kindly sent to us free by the Press of the State.

ADMIRAL RAPHAEL SEMMES BUILDING

This building contains the R. E. Lee, and Warfield memorial rooms.

Admiral Raphael Semmes was born in Charles County, Md., September 27th, 1809. He entered the U. S. Navy as Midshipman at the age of 17, was promoted to Lieut. ten years later, and rose to the rank of Commander at the age of 46. During the Mexican War he served on board ship and as an Aid to Gen'l Worth ; February 15th, 1861, at the outbreak he resigned the Secretaryship of the Light House Board at Washington, D. C., and took command of the Confederate steamer Sumter, at New Orleans, ran the blockade at the mouth of the Mississippi, and in July, 1861, captured a number of American vessels in the Gulf of Mexico. In August, 1862, he took command of the steamer Alabama ; he sunk the Hatteras, after a brief action, January, 1863, off Galveston. At the evacuation of Richmond, Admiral Semmes had charge of the James River Squadron. He surrendered at Greensboro, N. C., May 1st, 1865.

The following is a list of vessels captured and destroyed by Admiral Semmes.

Abbie Bradford.	Altamaha.	Emma Jane.	Nye.
Ben Danning.	Annie T. Schmidt.	Golden Rule.	Oemulgee.
Ebenezer Dodge.	Ben Tucker.	Jabez Snow.	Tonowonda.
Joseph Maxwell.	Charles Hill.	John A. Parks.	Parker Cook.
Machias.	Conrad.	Kingfisher.	Union Jack.
Neapolitan.	Dorcas Prince.	Lauretta.	Sea Bride.
Alert.	Emily Farnum.	Louisa Hatch.	Wave Crest.
Amazonian.	Golden Eagle.	Martaban.	Sonora.
Baron de Castine.	Hatteras.	Nora.	Starlight.
Brilliant.	Albert Adams.	Talisman.	Kate Cory.
Clara L. Sparks.	Dan'l Towbridge.	Olive Jane.	Lafayette-I.
Content.	Investigator.	Tycoon.	Levi Starbuck.
Elisha Dunbar.	Louis Killiam.	Punjab.	Martha Wenzell.
Express.	Naiad.	Virginia.	Nina.
Harriot Spalding.	West Wind.	Sea Lark.	Ocean Rover.
Arcade.	Amanda.	Weather Gage.	Thos. B. Wales.
Cuba.	Annie.	Justina.	Palmetto.
Golden Rocket.	Bertha Thayer.	Lamplighter.	Union.
Joseph Parks.	Chastelaine.	Lafayette.	Rockingham.
Montmorency.	Courser.	Manchester.	Washington.
Vigilance.	Dunkirk.	Winged Racer.	Morning Star. S. Gildersleeve.

GENL. ROBERT E. LEE MEMORIAL ROOM.

This room has been furnished through the liberality of the Brewers Exchange of Baltimore.

Wm. Miller, *President,*
Jno. P. Milnor, *Secretary,*
Paul A. Seger,   *Trustees,*
Fred. H. Gottleib,
Jno. Bauernschmidt, of Geo.

as a token of their appreciation of the Institution and of their admiration of the character of the great Commander.

The following tribute to the memory of Genl. Lee is from the late senator Benj. H. Hill, of Ga.

"When the future historian comes to survey the character of Lee, he will find it rising like a huge mountain above the undulating plain of humanity, and he will have to lift his eyes high toward heaven to catch its summit. He possessed every virtue of the other great commanders without their vices. He was a foe without hate, a friend without treachery, a soldier without cruelty and a victim without murmuring. He was a public officer without vices, a private citizen without wrong, a neighbor without reproach, a Christian without hypocrisy and a man without guilt. He was Cæsar without his ambition, Frederick without his tyranny, Napoleon without his selfishness and Washington without his reward. He was obedient to authority as a servant and royal in authority as a true king. He was as gentle as a woman in life, pure and modest as a virgin in thought, watchful as a Roman vestal in duty, submissive to law as Socrates, and grand in battle as Achilles."

THE WARFIELD ROOM.

This room has been furnished in memory of Albert Gallatin Warfield, Jr. and Gassaway Watkins Warfield, both members of Co. A, 1st Maryland Cavalry, C. S. A., by their mother and brothers Joshua N., Edwin, John and Marshall T. Warfield, and sisters, Mrs. M. Gillet Gill, of Baltimore, and Mrs. Herman Hoopes, of Philadelphia.

Albert Gallatin Warfield, Jr., was born at "Oakdale," Howard County, Maryland, October 6th, 1842, and died December 25th, 1883, (Christmas Day) in the 41st year of his age. He was the eldest son of Albert G. Warfield and Margaret Gassaway Watkins, daughter of Col. Gassaway Watkins of Revolutionary fame, who was the last surviving officer of the "Old Maryland Line," and at the time of his death in 1840, President of the Maryland Society of the Cincinnati. A. G. Warfield, Jr., was educated in the public schools and at Stanmore, an Academy under the management of the Hallowells. He left the Academy in the Summer of 1862 and entered the Confederate Army, joining Co. A, 1st Maryland Cavalry, under command of Col. Ridgely Brown. In the fall of that year he was stricken down with typhoid fever and lay ill at Winchester for many weeks. He was convalescing when the Confederates evacuated the town, but remained in hiding for ten days after the Federals arrived and tried in vain to escape. He gives in his diary, a most interesting account of the

experiences of himself and his companion Clark in their efforts to elude the Federal Soldiers and to escape, but finally, on December 27th, they were compelled to surrender. He was marched to Martinsburg, and from thence sent via the B. & O. to Camp Chase, Ohio. He was exchanged in the Spring of '63, after having been transferred to Fort McHenry, Baltimore, Md. He had not been with his regiment long, before he was sent on an important Scouting Expedition with five other picked men from his company, and with them was captured. This proved his greatest misfortune, as he was destined to spend two long dreary years in prison at Point Lookout. How this tried his patience and chafed his ambitious spirit, can best be told by his comrades in prison, W. H. Pope, Jas. R. Wheeler, and others. He made two daring and unsuccessful attempts to escape from Point Lookout. Mr. Pope, Superintendent of Confederate Soldiers' Home at Pikesville, speaking of his second attempt, said that he dug a tunnel from his tent to a point outside the prison pen, using nothing but a common pocket knife for the laborious and tedious work and carrying the earth excavated out in his pockets. After he had completed his tunnel and made all of his arrangements to carry out his plans he was betrayed and captured just as he emerged from the tunnel with his canoe built by himself, in which to cross the Potomac river. The Baltimore *American* of that date in describing the boat, and his effort to escape said : " It was built by the celebrated Rebel, Warfield, who has attempted to escape from the Camp before, and almost succeeded, but fortunately fell in with some of Uncle Sam's Cavalrymen and was ordered to halt, and not obeying, had a musket ball almost put through his head. It glanced along the top, slightly raising the scalp, and coming out behind the ear, without injury to the bone. He attempted to escape in the following manner : The Small-Pox Hospital is situated outside the picket lines, every day at three o'clock the Small-Pox Ambulance calls for those cases that have come to the knowledge of the Surgeons. Warfield had noticed the fact, and determined to try his luck in escaping, he procured a piece of wire, and by heating it red hot, succeeded in burning on his face a good many of the small papilla, which were taken for the regular varioloid, he succeeded in this manner in eluding the vigilance of the Surgeons and getting in the ambulance and outside the lines. As soon as he was out of sight of the camp, he slipped out of the ambulance and hid in the bushes, waited until dark, and then started for Dixie, and succeeded in getting some seven or eight miles when he fell in with some Federals who brought him to a halt, with the above result." These attempts to escape brought upon him many hardships and persecutions. In his letters he speaks of having been tied up by his thumbs in order to make him divulge the names of his comrades who aided and abetted him. He would have suffered death rather than betray a friend. His record in the prison camp at Point Lookout proved his gallantry and gave evidence of what he would have accomplished had he been allowed to serve in the field, the cause he so ardently espoused. He was brave and ambitious and would have won promotion had the opportunity been afforded him. He was finally exchanged the last of March, 1865, just before the close of the war. He gives in his diary an interesting account of his movements

from April 2nd, 1865, the day Richmond was evacuated, until he surrendered at Washington, Ga., May 9th, 1865. He speaks of Jefferson Davis being at Abbeville, May 2nd, 1865, and holding his last conference with Genls. T.C. Breckenridge, Bragg, Dibrell, and Col. W. P. C. Breckenridge. After his surrender he accompanied Genl. Basil Duke, Cols. Breckenridge, Steele and others to Savannah, where he embarked for home, reaching there June 2nd, 1865, after being absent three years in prison and the Confederacy. He remained home but a short time. Feeling that he must prepare himself for the real battle of life he decided upon Civil Engineering as his profession and began his studies under Mr. Benjamin Latrobe in the office of Smith & Latrobe, in Baltimore. After qualifying himself under the guidance of this distinguished engineer he entered upon the active pursuit of his profession in which he was engaged up to August 1883, when he was stricken down by the disease of which he died. His first work was upon the location of the Cincinnati and Louisville Short Line in 1868. After the completion of that line he went on the Pittsburg and Connellsville Railroad and remained until its completion as Assistant and Resident Engineer. In 1872 while acting as Chief Engineer of the Berlin branch of the P. & C. road, he was selected, upon the recommendation of Mr. Benjamin H. Latrobe, who always entertained a high opinion of his ability as engineer to the Scientific Commission which went to Japan with Genl. Horace Capron as Chief. The work of the Commission included the examination of the country with reference to the introduction of railroads and other improved means of transportation, and this branch was confined to Mr. Warfield. He remained in Japan three years, and desiring to travel through the East and Europe, he declined to renew his contract with the Government. He spent a year travelling through Asia, Africa and Europe, visiting all of the great engineering works in those countries and other points of interest. Upon his return he was selected by a Committee of Congress to inspect the Mississippi jetties and river, and to make a report upon the same, which he did, and it was endorsed by the Committee and incorporated in the report of the Chairman to Congress. In the fall of 1876 he entered the service of the Southern Pacific Railroad, where he remained until 1880, except for a period of one year, when he acted as Assistant State Engineer of California, in charge of the surveys of the Sacramento and San Joaquin Rivers for the purpose of establishing irrigation. He also located a road in the beautiful Yosemite Valley. Preferring to live in his native State, he resigned from the service of the Southern Pacific Railroad in 1880, and returned to Maryland. He entered the service of the B. & O. Railroad, in the road department, and while with that Company was detailed to locate the Baltimore end of its Philadelphia extension and some branch roads for the Company in Virginia. He afterwards became Chief Engineer of the West Virginia Central and Pittsburg Railroad, and remained with it until he was forced to resign by his fatal illness. The disease from which he died was aneurism of the Aorta and it was supposed to have been superinduced by the exposure of prison life during the war. He left surviving him a widow and three children, one boy and two daughters.

SOUTHERN VIEW OF HOME.

ENTRANCE LOUDON PARK CEMETERY.

CONFEDERATE GRAVES, LOUDON PARK CEMETERY.

Loudon Park Cemetery.

One of the most Modern and Beautiful Cemeteries in the
. . . . Country. . . . .

REACHED EVERY FEW MINUTES

By Baltimore & Potomac, and
Catonsville Steam and Horse
Cars. ∴ ∴ ∴ ∴

→✳View of New Entrance and Confederate Lot✳←
ON OPPOSITE PAGE.

*The great number of Sections "Laid off" affords a large and
varied selection of Choice Lots to Purchasers.*

Mausoleum

For the Use of Lotholders, is a substantial and beautiful
. Temporary Home for the Dead.

☞The Superintendent on the grounds will give all information as to Lots, etc.

Gassaway Watkins Warfield was the third son of Albert G. and Margaret G. Warfield, and was born at Oakdale, Howard county, Md., November 29th, 1846. When the Civil War began he was in his fifteenth year. The one desire and ambition of his youth was to be a soldier and fight for the Southern Cause. He was sent to Rock Hill College in 1861, and continued there until July, 1864. During his college life he longed to go South, and then decided to do so when an opportunity offered. This came soon after his return home for his summer vacation in 1864, when Gen. Early invaded Maryland. Notwithstanding the fact that the hope of success of the Confederate cause was fast waning, his patriotic ardor won, and he cast his lot with the forlorn hope of the Rebels. On the 11th of July, 1864, he buckled on his sword, donned the grey, bade farewell to home and dear ones, and with a mother's prayers and benedictions, rode off to do battle for the cause that he believed to be right and just. He enlisted in Co. A., 1st Maryland Cavalry, C. S. A., at Triadelphia. The company was then under command of the gallant Capt. Thos. Griffith. Young Warfield's career as a soldier in active service in the field was brief, lasting but twenty-six days, yet it was one filled with exciting incidents, forced marches and almost daily fighting.

Mr. Trusten Polk, who was a member of Co. A, gives the following interesting account of the movements of his regiment from July 11th, 1864, until its capture, August 6th. He says: "On July 12th met Federal cavalry at Bladensburg, and pursued them to within one mile of Washington City. We then took a road to Point Lookout, intending to liberate the Confederate prisoners, but were recalled by Gen. Early, who was bombarding Washington. July 13 commenced retreating and recrossed the Potomac near Poolesville, under heavy fire from Federal cavalry, then marched to Hedgesville, Berkley county, Va., and, after resting a few days, started on a raid into Pennsylvania, fighting incessantly day and night until we passed through Washington county, Md. Encountered but few Federal soldiers in Pennsylvania. Burned Chambersburg in retaliation for the burning done in the Valley by Hunter. Returned to West Virginia by way of New Creek Station (now Keyser), and attempted to capture the town, but were repulsed by Federal artillery. We then crossed the mountains by way of Romney to Moorefield, and there halted to rest in a beautiful meadow on the celebrated McNeil estate. We had had no sleep or rest since leaving Hedgesville—seven days— except what was snatched by laying our heads on the necks of our horses. On the morning of August 6th, 1864, at dawn of day, we were awakened by Federal cavalry, under command of Gen. Averill, and made prisoners of war without firing a shot—virtually caught napping. We were marched on foot back to New Creek Station, and next day sent to Wheeling, where we were quartered in the penitentiary for three days and then sent to Camp Chase, Ohio. Thus young Gassaway Watkins Warfield rounded up his brief career in the field as a soldier. The exposure and hardships of prison life soon told upon his youthful constitution, and he was stricken down with a fatal fever in October, and, after long suffering, he died January 14th, 1865, a martyr to the cause he loved and for which he freely gave up his life. His prison comrades, realizing that he could not recover if

he remained in prison, wrote his father, urging him to take steps to procure his release. This he did, but found that it could only be accomplished by the prisoner taking the oath of allegiance to the United States. This young Warfield refused to do, notwithstanding the pleadings of his father and friends in prison. To their entreaties he replied that he would rather die than sacrifice his principles and forsake the cause he had espoused. His remains were brought to his home in Maryland, and now rest under the sod of his native State, with those of his brother, who served the lost cause with him.

His messmates in prison were Trusten Polk, Wm. A. Webb, Edwin Linthicum, Chas. C. Hutton, Thomas Hunter, Thomas Peters, Josiah Slingluff, George Rice, B. E. Peddicord and Frank Lipscomb.

MAJOR GEN. ARNOLD ELZEY BUILDING.

This building contains the Quartermaster's Department, Pharmacy, and the Superintendent's Office.

This distinguished officer was Captain 2nd Artillery, and in command of the U. S. Arsenal, Augusta, Ga., when he resigned in the early part of 1861. On June 19th, 1861, he was commissioned Colonel 1st Maryland Infantry. Upon the disablement of Gen. E. Kirby Smith, at the head of this regiment, July 21st, 1861, moving into position on the memorable field of Manassas, the command of the brigade devolved upon Col. Elzey, who successfully continued the movement and assailed the enemy with such vigor as to cause them to give way; this retreat soon became a panic, and the result was the complete rout of the Federal Army. At this moment President Davis rode over the field and, meeting Col. Elzey, saluted him as "General," remarking, "You are the 'Blucher of the day.'"

Gen. Elzey remained in command of this brigade until made a major-general and assigned to command of the defenses at Richmond in December, 1862.

At Cross Keys, in June, 1862, he rendered valuable service, the position occupied by the Confederate forces was of his selection, and Gen. Ewell, in his report, says: "I availed myself frequently during the action of that officer's counsel, profiting largely by his known military skill and judgment; he was much exposed, his horse was wounded early in the action, and at a later period of the day, was killed by a rifle ball, which at the same time inflicted upon the rider a wound that forced him to retire from the field; he was more particularly employed in the centre directing the artillery."

Gen. Elzey was seriously wounded at Gaines' Mill, June 27th, 1862, in which battle his brigade took active part and sustained heavy loss. His ability as a soldier was recognized by Gen. Lee, who suggested to the President he should order him to take the field in January, 1863. Again, in May, 1863, Gen. Lee wrote to President Davis, that he greatly needed two major-generals, and asked that Gen. Elzey be sent to him to command Trimble's Division.

April 25th, 1864, Gen. Elzey was ordered to Staunton to establish headquarters as Commander of the Maryland Line; September 8th, 1864, was assigned to duty as Chief of Artillery in the Army of Tennessee.

OFFICE OF SUPERINTENDENT.

The Superintendent's Office contains the usual office furniture, with the following pictures and muster rolls, framed, hanging on the wall: "Prayer in Stonewall Jackson's Camp," "The Charge of the First Maryland Infantry at Harrisonburg, Va., at the death of Ashby," "Last Meeting of Lee and Jackson," "Muster Rolls of Co. A, First Maryland Infantry, and Co. D, First Maryland Cavalry," "Letter from Jefferson Davis, Camp St. Mary, or Camp of the Maryland Line at Hanover Junction, January, 1864," and several others.

QUARTERMASTER'S ROOM.

The Quartermaster's Department is fitted up with shelves and such other conveniences as are required. Everything is given out here that is required in the different departments, from a needle up to a uniform. Tobacco day is looked for with fond anticipation. On one side of the room are the bins which hold the linen of the memorial rooms. The linen is brought here and stored until issued for use. There is an inspector who takes an account of all the linen coming out of the rooms. On Monday morning a clerk takes an account of all going into the laundry; a perfect system is maintained, so that everything will be properly accounted for. W. H. Davies is Quartermaster for the Home.

MEDICAL DEPARTMENT.

Wm. P. E. Wyse, M. D. - - Surgeon to the Home.
Benj. Gough, M. D. - - Pharmacist.
B. R. Jennings, D. D. S. - - Dentist.

CONSULTING SURGEONS.

Dr. Chas. G. Hill,   Dr. Thomas S. Latimer,
Dr. E. E. Jones,   Dr. J. J. Chisholm.

CONSULTING DENTIST.

Dr. R. B. Winder.

The Surgeon's Office, dispensary, and the Stonewall Jackson Infirmary are the chief points of interest in the Medical Department of the home. Those patients able to get about report to the Surgeon's Office where they are treated. The less fortunate ones, who are too sick to report at the Surgeon's Office, are sent to the Infirmary, where they are under the care of skilled nurses and visited by the Surgeon every day, or oftener, if necessary.

GENL. E. KIRBY SMITH ROOM. (PHARMACY.)

The Surgeon's Office and Dispensary are situated on the East end of the Elzey Building, and is one of the prettiest and most attractive places within the walls of the Home, which is due to the liberality and good taste of Mrs. Decatur H. Miller, who recently fitted up and furnished it at considerable expense. It is carpeted, the wood work of highly polished hand carved oak, and medicine case of same wood. Under a brass chandelier, a handsome centre table has upon it a silver waiter, ice water

pitcher and goblets, which are decidedly useful as well as ornamental, all combine to make the Surgeon's Office a cheery place of refuge for those who require the aid of the healing art.

Mrs. Miller has indicated her wish that this room be named in memory of the late Genl. E. Kirby Smith. Genl. Smith was an officer of distinguished reputation in the United States Army, when his duty to his State prompted him to resign his commission at the commencement of the war. He was appointed a Brigadier General, and ordered to report to Genl. Joseph E. Johnston, commanding the Army of the Shenandoah, in July, 1861, and was severely wounded at the first Battle of Manassas, leading his brigade into action. Genl. Smith afterwards was made a Major General and assigned to a Division under General Johnston, but was subsequently transferred to the Armies of the West, and finally was in command of the Department of the Trans-Mississippi. The services of General Smith in this command were of great importance, and added to his already high reputation as an able soldier. It devolved upon him to make surrender of the last army of the Confederacy, when he returned to civil life, and, like the immortal Lee, his honored Chieftain, devoted himself to the education of the youth of his country. At the time of his death, March 28th, 1893, he was connected with the University of the South, Sewanee, Tenn. Genl. Smith attained the rank of full General in the Confederate Service.

BRIGADIER GENERAL CHAS. S. WINDER BUILDING.

The rooms in this building are the Dining, or Mess Hall, the Commissary Department and the Kitchen.

The Mess Hall is 46x18 feet, contains four large tables and Chairs; it is in charge of a detail, consisting of sergeant and five men, who attend to it and keep it in order. This room was furnished by Lieut. Geo. W. Wood of Baltimore. Lieut. Wood, prior to the war, lived in Louisiana and served with troops from that State.

The Commissary Department occupies two small rooms and is in charge of Richard C. Briscoe, the Commissary.

The Kitchen is on the same floor and convenient to the Mess Hall.

GENL. WINDER was educated at West Point, appointed 2nd Lieutenant of Infantry and afterwards promoted to be 1st Lieutenant, and was ordered to the Pacific Coast. The Steamer "San Francisco," on which the troops took passage from New York, was disabled by a hurricane, off the Atlantic coast and, drifting helpless for many days before the storm, was reported lost for several weeks. Different vessels rescued the crew and passengers, however, and Lieut. Winder and his men, whom he refused to leave, were taken to Liverpool. For his conduct on this occasion, he was promoted to be Captain in the 9th Regiment Infantry, being, it is believed, the youngest captain in the army. He was again ordered to the Pacific coast and, with his company, took part in Steptoe's Campaign against the Columbia River Indians, being present at his defeat and perilous retreat under cover of night. He also took part in Colonel Wright's subsequent successful campaign against the same Indians.

Early in 1861 he resigned his command and offered his services to the Confederate Government at Montgomery, and was commissioned Captain

in the regular C. S. Army. Being ordered to Charleston, he was present at the reduction of Fort Sumter. He was afterwards in the command of the South Carolina Arsenal, until commissioned Colonel of the 6th South Carolina Infantry, arriving with his regiment at Manassas just at the close of the battle of July 21st; March 4, 1862, nominated by President Davis to be a Brigadier General; March 25th, 1862, assigned to the command of the 4th Brigade, Hill's Division, but without taking command, was on the emergency of a vacancy in the command of the Stonewall Brigade, assigned to the same and participated in the Valley Campaign of 1862; August 1862 assigned to command of Jackson's Division; was mortally wounded whilst in command of this Division, August 9th, 1862, at Cedar Mountain. Genl. Winder was engaged in the battles of McDowell, Gaines' Mill, Malvern Tavern, Winchester, Harper's Ferry, Port Republic, Cedar Mountain and others.

Gen. T. J. Jackson, in his report of the battle of Cold Harbor, says: "In pursuance of the order to charge the enemy's front, the First Virginia brigade, commanded by Gen. C. S. Winder, moved forward through the swamp, and upon emerging into the open fields, its ranks broken by the obstacles encountered, were re-formed, meeting at that point with the Hampton Legion, First Maryland, 12th Alabama, 52nd Virginia, and 38th Georgia, they were formed upon his line. Thus formed they moved forward under the lead of that gallant officer, whose conduct here was marked by the coolness and courage which distinguished him on the battle-fields of the Valley."

Genl. Robert E. Lee, in his report of the Battle of Cedar Mountain, says: "I can add nothing to the well-deserved tribute paid to the courage, capacity, and conspicuous merit of this lamented officer, by Genl. Jackson, in whose brilliant campaign in the Valley and on the Chickahominy, he bore a distinguished part."

Genl. T. J. Jackson, in his report of the same battle, says, "He was proceeding to direct, with his usual skill and coolness, the movements of these batteries, when he was struck by a shell, from which he expired in a few hours. It is difficult within the proper reserve of an official report to do justice to the merits of this accomplished officer. Urged by the medical director to take no part in the movements of the day, because of the enfeebled state of his health, his ardent patriotism and military pride could bear no such restraint; richly endowed with those qualities of mind and person which fit an officer for command, and which attract the admiration and excite the enthusiasm of troops, he was rapidly rising to the front rank of his profession, and his loss has been severely felt."

THE BRIGADIER GENERAL WILLIAM W. MACKALL BUILDING.

This building is to the left of the entrance, and is occupied by the Superintendent and family. It was occupied in 1861 by Genl. Huger, just before he resigned and entered the service of the Confederacy.

Genl. W. W. Mackall, of Cecil County, Md., on September 15th, 1861, was Lieut. Col. A. A. G., and Chief of Staff of Genl. Albert Sydney

Howard Auditorium.

JAMES L. KERNAN, - - - Owner and Manager.

BALTIMORE'S FAMILY VAUDEVILLE RESORT.

For Ladies and Children.

PRESENTING COMEDY AND HIGH CLASS VAUDEVILLE ATTRACTIONS.

Theatre equipped with every convenience contributing to the Comfort of Patrons.

MATINEES DAILY.

Prices, 15, 25, 50 and 75 cents.   Box Seats, $1.

CHILDREN'S MATINEE TICKETS, 10 cents.

Kernan's Monumental Theatre.

JAMES L KERNAN, - - Proprietor and Manager.

BALTIMORE'S HOME OF VAUDEVILLE.

PRESENTING HIGH CLASS SPECIALTY ATTRACTIONS ONLY.

Spacious Annex in Rear of Theatre, provided with BOWLING ALLEYS AND POOL TABLES.

Matinees Tuesday, Thursday and Saturday.

Night Prices,   10, 25, 50 and 75 cts. Box Seats, $1.
Matinee Prices,   10, 25, and 50 cts. Box Seats, $1.

Holliday=St. Theatre.

KERNAN, RIFE & HOUCK, - - - Proprietors.
GEO. W. RIFE, - - Manager.

Matinees Monday, Wednesday & Saturday.

DRAMA, COMEDY, MINSTRELS.

Modern Equipment.   Perfect Exits.   Centrally Located.

Night Prices, 15, 25, 50 and 75 cts.   Box Seats, $1.
Matinee Prices,   15, 25 and 50 cts.   Box Seats, $1.

RALEIGH C. THOMAS MEMORIAL HALL AND LIBRARY.

COL. HARRY GILMOR ROOM.

Johnson; March 4th, 1862, nominated by President Davis as Brigadier General-; March 26th, 1862, by Special Orders No. 445, Headquarters Grand Division, Army of the Mississippi, dated Corinth, Miss., was ordered to the command of the Confederate forces at Madrid Bend and Island No. 10; October 14th, 1862, by Special Orders No. 240, War Department, ordered to report for duty to Major Genl. Samuel Jones, commanding Department of Tennessee; December 14th, 1862, assigned to the command or the District of the Gulf; February 1st, 1863, Brig. Gen. in command of Western Division, District of the Gulf, Major General S. B. Buckner commanding; April 17th, 1863, by General Orders No. 9, announced as Chief of Staff, Department No. 2, Braxton Bragg commanding; October 16th, 1863, by General orders No. 2, Department of Tennessee, relieved as Chief of Staff; November 4th, 1863, by Special Orders No. 235, Headquarters, Department of Mississippi and East Louisiana, assigned to the command of the Brigades, lately commanded by Brig. Genl. Herbert; January 26th, 1864, by General Orders No. 6, Department of Tennessee, announced as Chief of Staff to Genl. Joseph E. Johnston; July 24th, 1864, by Special Field Orders No. 56, Headquarters Army of Tennessee, relieved from duty as Chief of Staff at his own request.

Brig. Genl. W. W. Mackall was engaged in the Battle of Madrid Bend and Island No. 10, April 1-6, 1862, at which time he was captured, Genl. Beauregard in a letter to Genl. S. Cooper, dated Jackson, Tenn., February 24th, 1862, says: "The services of Col. Mackall as a division commander I consider indispensable at this critical juncture. My health is such as to make it essential for me to have as many trained experienced officers to aid me as practicable."

Genl. Beauregard, in a letter to Mackall, dated August 22d, 1862, says: "I am happy to hear of your safe return to the Confederacy, and hope you will soon receive a command commensurate with your merit. . . . I hope to report for duty on or about the 1st, proximo, when I would be most happy to have you under my orders should you desire to serve under me again."

Genl. Saml. Jones, in a letter to the Secretary of War, dated October 14th, 1862, says: "I telegraphed you on the 12th instant to say that I needed the services of a Brigadier General to this department (East Tennessee), and that if you thought proper to order Brig. General Mackall, who I understand is without a Brigade, to report to me, I should be glad to have him." .

J. G. Shorter, Governor of Alabama, in a letter dated May 6th, 1863, to the Secretary of War, says: "I telegraphed you to-day that the citizens of Mobile desired the assignment of Brig. General Mackall to the command in that city. . . . I need not remind you of the vital importance of assigning to such a high position of responsibility an officer of skill and energy, and whose qualifications will command the respect and confidence of the citizens of Mobile and the authorities of Alabama."

In General Orders No. 2, dated October 16th, 1863, General Bragg says: "At his request, Brig. General W. W. Mackall is relieved from duty as Chief of Staff with the commanding General of the army. He

will proceed with his aids and report to Genl. J. E. Johnston, now commanding the Department from which he was transferred. With a grateful sense of the distinguished services rendered by this accomplished officer in the high position he has filled, the commanding General tenders him his cordial thanks and wishes him all success and happiness in his future career. The General and the Army will long feel the sacrifice made in sparing the services of one so distinguished for capacity, professional acquirements and urbanity."

General Leonidas Polk, in a letter to Genl. J. E. Johnston, dated January 5th, 1864, says: "I will return you Forney or M. L. Smith or Mackall, with the recommendation of the latter for Major General."

STONEWALL JACKSON INFIRMARY.

The necessity of a Hospital Building, detached from the living rooms at the Home, was early demonstrated. A building, which in the days of the Arsenal was used as a Laboratory, was made available for this purpose. It is a substantial structure, removed some 100 yards or more from the other buildings, and was fitted up for Hospital use through the efforts of Mrs. J. H. Tegmyer, Mrs. R. B. Winder, Mrs. Harvey Jones, Mrs. J. H. Harris, Mrs. M. B. Brown, Mrs. John Brosius and their associates. The room is fitted up with four beds, and has been found a great comfort. It has been named after the immortal Jackson, whose military genius was only equalled by his unshrinking faith and consistent Christian character. With him the watchword of life was comprehended in one word—"duty." Wherever he recognized this principle his devotion was complete, whether it called him to face the dangers of battle in his country's service, or whether it led him to humbler, but no less noble deeds in the service of his God. His submission to the will of his Maker and recognition of Divine Providence in all things, both small and great, was as marked as those great abilities which made him the military hero of the war.

LIST OF OFFICERS

OF THE

Maryland Line Confederate Soldiers' Home.

WM. H. POPE,	Superintendent.
DR. W. P. E. WYSE,	Surgeon.
BENJAMIN GOUGH,	Asst. Surgeon.
CHARLES W. SEMMES,	Adjutant.
WM. H. DAVIES,	Quartermaster.
RICHARD C. BRISCOE,	Commissary.
B. R. JENNINGS,	Inspector.
MATTHEW GREEN,	Librarian.

RULES.

1st. Uniforms must be worn on Sundays, holidays, and all other occasions when the Superintendent may direct.

2d. No member of the Home will be permitted to leave the grounds unless by the consent of the Superintendent.

3d. Use of liquors especially prohibited, unless by Surgeon's order.

4th. Quarreling and boisterous behavior are strictly prohibited.

5th. Any complaints from the members of the Home shall be in writing, and forwarded through the Superintendent to the Board of Managers.

In addition to the foregoing the Superintendent is directed to raise the National and State colors on all public occasions. The flag staff at the Home is 138 feet high, perhaps the tallest in the State, and cost $500, the principal part of which expense was personally borne by James R. Wheeler, Esq., Chairman of the Managers.

Maryland Line, Hanover Junction, Va.

WINTER, 1863-4.

After the return of the Army to the lines of the Rappahannock and Rapidan Rivers, in the fall of 1863, the Maryland Line was detached and assembled at Hanover Junction, Va., and charged with the duty of protecting that depot and the bridges over the North and South Anna Rivers, which in that neighborhood unite and form the Pamunkey. This post being on the direct line over which General Lee drew his supplies and maintained his communication with Richmond, was of great importance, and in addition to its defence, the country below Richmond lying to the north of the Richmond and York River R. R., was also held under observation and thoroughly picketed. The service rendered during this winter was of signal value, not only to the preservation of the line of communication of the Army, but also in the defense of Richmond, which during this period was several times threatened by the Federal forces operating on the Peninsula and by cavalry raids, among the latter the notable Kilpatrick-Dalgren expedition. The commands of the Maryland Line thus assembled for this duty were the

FIRST MARYLAND CAVALRY,
SECOND MARYLAND INFANTRY,
FIRST MARYLAND ARTILLERY (Dement),
SECOND MARYLAND ARTILLERY (Baltimore Light),
FOURTH MARYLAND ARTILLERY (Chesapeake).

The Line, Field and Staff was as follows:

BRADLEY T. JOHNSON,	Colonel Commanding.
GEO. W. BOOTH,	Capt. and A. A. G.
WILSON C. NICHOLAS,	Capt. and A. I. G.
GEO. H. KYLE,	Major and C. S.
CHAS. W. HARDING,	Major and Q. M.
RICHARD P. JOHNSON,	Surgeon.
REV. THOMAS DUNCAN,	Chaplain.

Muster Rolls
Maryland Line P. A. of the Confederate States.

These rolls have been compiled from original muster rolls found in the War Record Office, Washington, D. C., but are incomplete. For several Companies no rolls whatever have been found, and in no instance was a complete set obtainable.

FIRST REGIMENT, MARYLAND INFANTRY.

FIELD AND STAFF.

COLONELS.

ARNOLD ELZEY, June 17th, 1861.
Promoted Brigadier-General July 21st, 1861.
Promoted Major-General December 4th, 1862.

GEORGE H. STEUART, July 21st, 1861.
Promoted Brigadier-General March 18th, 1862.

BRADLEY T. JOHNSON, March 18th, 1862.
Promoted Brigadier-General June 28th, 1864.

LIEUT-COLONELS,

GEORGE H. STEUART, June 17, 1861.   E. R. DORSEY, March 18, 1862.
BRADLEY T. JOHNSON, July 21, 1861.

MAJORS,

BRADLEY T. JOHNSON, June 17, 1861.   E. R. DORSEY, July 21, 1861.

ACTING ADJUTANTS,

LIEUT. FRANK X. WARD, Co. H.   LIEUT. GEO. W. BOOTH, Co. D.

SURGEONS,

E. T. GALLIARD.   R. P. JOHNSON.

ASSISTANT SURGEONS,

STYLES KENNEDY.   THOS. S. LATIMER.

CAPTAIN and A. Q. M.,

GRAFTON D. SPURRIER.   SEPTIMUS H. STEWART.
CHAS. W. HARDING.

CAPTAIN and A. C. S.,

JOHN E. HOWARD.

CHAPLAIN,

STEPHEN J. CAMERON.

SERGEANT-MAJOR,

GEO. W. BISHOP.
PHILIP L. MOORE.

Q. M. SERGEANT,

CHAS. J. WEGNER.

CHIEF MUSICIAN,

ALEX. HUBBARD.

DRUM MAJOR,

HOSEA PITT.

MESS HALL.

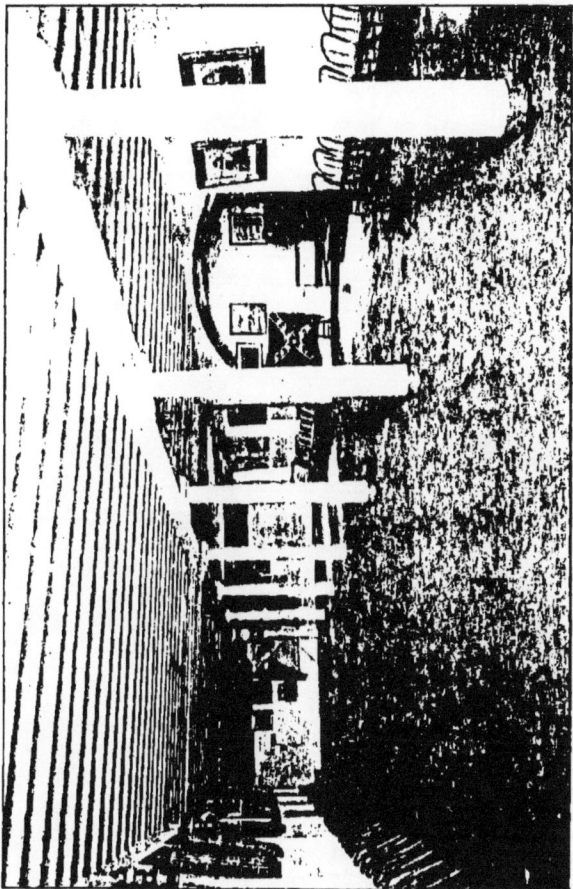

Relic Hall.

Co. A.

Bradley T. Johnson, Capt.
Wm. W. Goldsborough, Capt.
Geo. K. Shellman, 1st Lieut.
Chas. W. Blair, 2nd Lieut.
Geo. M. E. Shearer, 2nd Lieut.
W. H. B. Dorsey, 2nd Lieut.
John F. Groshon, 1st Sergt.
John T. Smith, Sergt.

Geo. Tyler, Sergt.
D. Windsor Kessler, Sergt.
W. H. Pope, Sergt.
Francis T. Bender, Corp.
Wm. Ritter, Corp.
Perry McDowell, Corp.
Jas. Abbott, Corp.
Alex. J. Hubbard, Musician.

PRIVATES.

Ackhurst, Chas.
Agen, Peter
Andre, Jno. A.
Bowers, Cornelius
Brown, John W.
Bush, Geo. W.
Bride, Sam'l
Butler, Cyrus S.
Bryan, Sam'l
Bobeth, Chas.
Bond, B. F.
Cook, Wm.
Chizzler, Henry
Carlick, Jno.
Chambers, Robt. M.
Conrad, Geo.
Callan, Jno.
Carey, Timothy
Foreman, Valentine
Gephart, Sol. A.
Geasey, Jas. W.
Goldsborough, N. Lee
Grove, Louis
Goldsborough
Hahn, Reuben H.
Hecht, Robt. H.

Hastings, Hugh
Heck, Jacob
Hewes, James
Hoppell, Geo. W.
Hammel, Edward
Hill, Jno. A.
Hazell, Patrick
Hamilton, Edward
Harding, Chas. W.
Hildt, Jno.
Kretzer, Hiram
Kennedy, Arthur T.
Lechlider, Thos. G.
Lechlider, Geo.
Loveley, Jno. E.
Lanahan, Daniel
Lartz, Nicholas
Lawson, Jas. A.
McMahan, Francis
McMullin, Chas.
McLanahan, W. H.
McLaughlin, Thos. G.
Mayberry, Jas. P.
Maguire, Geo. W.
Mallen, Henry
Myers, Christeso P.

Mindham, John
Mewberne, Matth. J.
Miles, Geo. T.
Moore, Philip L.
Owens, Sam'l A.
Oates, Chas. T.
O'Connell, Patrick
Porter, Hugh
Peters, Andrew
Rider, Martin L.
Ritter, Wm.
Ryan, W. H.
Rosenthal, Jas.
Steele, Jno. H.
Street, Jno. H.
Strickland, Jesse
Swisher, Jno.
Stewart, Edward B.
Snovell, D. M.
Tyler, Jno. E.
Taylor, Jno. B.
Williams, Edward
Wheeler, Chas. W.
Wever, Hiram
Wentz, Louis

Co. B.

Chas. C. Edelin, Capt.
Jas. Mullen, 1st Lieut.
Thos. Costello, 2nd Lieut.
Jos. Griffin, 2nd Lieut.
Peter Boyle, 1st Sergt.
Geo. Moog, Sergt.
Daniel Dougherty, Sergt.

Jas. Lemates, Sergt.
Geo. Bates, Corp.
Wm. Haffey, Corp.
Dennis O'Brian, Corp.
Geo. Probest, Corp.
Joseph Smith, Musician.

PRIVATES.

Abel, Chas.
Amey, Chas.
Bromley, Oram J.
Bruner, Hamilton
Bremer, Jno. L.
Chaney, Wm.
Chenoweth, Joseph
Cusick, Frederick
Cain, Jno.
Carey, Michael
Crenshaw, Wm.
Dopman, Chas.

Durkin, John
Dammen, Jos.
Disney, Wm.
Eckhart, Aug.
Flanagan, Jefferson
Gilland, Stephen
Gavin, Wm.
Glenon, Jno.
Hummel, Joseph
Heimiller, Herman
Haffey, Jno.
Hissey, Jno.

Hircht, Albert
Jones, Wm.
Kliser, Aug.
Kavladge, Jno.
Kries, Geo.
Kenney, Bernard
Kelley, Stewart
Kohlhepp, Jno.
Lutz, Conrad.
Lowe, Dan'l W.
Moog, Jas. R.
Miller, Wm. H.

McCall, Alexander
McGee, Dan'l
McGee, Jno.
Mannen, Bartley
Murray, Jno.
Murray, Thos.
McLaughlin, Martin
Mitchell, James
Michaels, Jno.
Michaels, Jos.
Moore, Robert
Micou, Thos.
Noonan, Michael

Opel, Jno.
O'Neal, Patrick
O'Neal, Andrew
Patton, Wm.
Plant, Augustus
Reynolds, Patrick
Ryan, Patrick
Rhodes, Geo.
Rush, Peter.
Shultz, Wm.
Sims, Jos.
Smith, Frederick
Schaeffer, Wm.

Shockney, Sam'l
Sherman, Robt. T
South, Howard
Stiteler, Chas. B.
Stephens, Jno.
Tyler, Wm.
Wentworth, Geo.
Wolf, Jos.
Wild, Geo.
Welsh, Jas.
Weaver, Geo.
Wilson.

Co. C.

Robt. C. Smith, Capt.
Septimus H. Stewart, 1st Lieut.
Wm. P. Thomas, 2nd Lieut.
Wm. Smyth, 1st Sergt.
Sterling Murray, Sergt.
Jno. B. Berryman, Sergt.

Jno. H. Welborn, Sergt.
Chas. A. Arnold, Corp.
Jno. O'Loughlin, Corp.
Frank S. Price, Corp.
Henry C. Scott, Corp.
Hosea Pitt, Musician.

PRIVATES.

Anderson, Jas.
Arnold, Frank A.
Arnold, Sam'l
Barry, Dan'l R.
Berry, Jno. P.
Bussey, Thos. J.
Conrad, Christian J.
Culbreth, Jno.
Codd, W. H.
Delevie, Jacob
Duck, Henry R. S.
Feast, Loudon
Fitzgerald, Wm. B.
Falconer, Edward W.
Flack, Thos. J. A.
Guise, Andrew
Gassaway, Sam'l
Golder, Hamilton
Grogan, Kennedy
Glaudel, Jno.
Hayden, Rich'd A.
Howard, Edward L.
Howard, Jas. McHenry

Hyland, Jno. G.
Hopkins, Henry H.
Hartmier, Rich'd J.
Infoes, Alfred I.
Johnston, Philip P.
Johnson, Jno. W.
Johannes, Martin J.
Johnson, Rich'd P.
Kane, Jas. C.
Latimer, Geo. S.
Latimer, Thos. S.
Lepper, Chas. V.
Murray, Wm. H.
Morgan, Benj. H.
McCabe, Geo. W. E.
McClernand, Jas.
Montgomery, Wm. T.
Maguire, Jas. W.
Norfolk, W. H.
Osburn, Jas. E.
Postley, Chas. T.
Perregoy, Jno. T.
Pue, Wm. H.

Rogers, Jno. C.
Rinehart, Wm.
Reinhart.
Slater, Geo.
Sisson, Oscar B.
Sloan, Chas. H.
Scott, Chas. A.
Smith, Thos. J.
Rogers, Wm. H.
Thomas, Dan'l L.
Thornton, Frank A.
Tongue, Rich'd H.
Tippett.
Voss, Franklin
Wilson, Chas. G.
White, Fisher A.
White, David D.
West, Geo. F.
Watkins, Jno.
Welch, Jno. L.
Walsh, Thos. K.
Warhen, Dan'l

Co. D.

Jas. R. Herbert, Capt.
Geo. W. Booth, 1st Lieut.
Wm. Key Howard, 2nd Lieut.
Nicholas Snowden, 2nd Lieut.
Geo. F. Ruff, 1st Sergt.
Chas. J. Wegner, Sergt.
Wm. H. Slingluff, Sergt.
Edward L. King, Sergt.

Mason E. McKnew, Sergt.
Edward Selvage, Corp.
Jos. Wranck, Corp.
Washington Hands, Corp.
Wm. Weber, Corp.
Chas. Tuttle, Musician.
Jas. M. Ruley, Musician.

PRIVATES.

Auuen, Henry
Ackler, Wm.
Ashton, J. J.
Bull, Jno. E.

Baker, Henry
Boyd, Hamilton
Berry, Thos. S.
Beatty, Edw. W.

Brown, Wm.
Briddle, Jas.
Bird, Chas. E.
Creamer, Jacob I.

Collins, Jno. W.
Conn, Wm. D.
Coyle, Patrick
Connelly, Edward T.
Devitt, Edward I.
Dashield, Geo. H.
Duvall, Ridgely
Edell, Henry
Edwards, Wm. H.
Enow, Chas. E.
Ferrell, Thos.
Gray, Wm. R.
Green, Hugh T.
Green, Matthew
Howard, Jno. E.
Hill, Wm.
Hendorf, Fred'k
Hitzelberger, Chas. T.
Holbrook, Jno. F.
Heimiller, Wm.
Howard, Chas.
Jennings, Benj. R.

Jenkins, Wm.
Jones, Jno. T.
Jones, John.
Key, Jno. R.
Key, D. Murray·
Knox, Jas.
Knox, Richard
Kelton, Jno.
Kueller, Jacob S.
Kelly, Jas. S.
King, Walter
Larrabee, Geo. S.
League, Jno. S.
Lowndes, Jas. A.
McKenna, Peter
McCann, Wm.
Murphy, Edward
McIntyre, Jos.
McIntyre, Rob't
McNulty, Jas.
Muth, Alfred
Norton, Jno. J.

O'Loughlin, Michael
O'Neil, Jno.
O'Brien, Edwin
Perry, Oliver
Rogers, Henry C.
Robinson, Wm. H.
Ryan, Rob't S.
Ray, Alex.
Spurrier, Jay
Small, C. W.
Soiskey, Isadore
Simpson, Joshua
Simon, August
Simms, Jno.
Taliaferro, Jno. R.
Travers, Jno. M.
Wells, Herschel
Wilson, Wm. A.
Wilson, Jno. A.
Weeks, Henry
Wegner, Henry F.
Whitely, Rob't M.

Co. E.

Edmund O'Brien, Capt.
Jno. J. Lutts, 1st Lieut.
Jno. Cushing, Jr., 2nd Lieut.
Jos. G. W. Marriott, 2nd Lieut.
Geo. G. Raborg, 1st Sergt.
Napoleon Camper, Sergt.
Green H. Barton, Sergt.
Wm. T. Wallis, Sergt.

Rob't H. Cushing, Sergt.
Patrick H. Williams, Corp.
Thos. H. Davidson, Corp.
Joseph T. Doyle, Corp.
Alfred Pearce, Corp.
Wm. Gannon, Musician.
Michael Quinn, Musician.

PRIVATES.

Adams, Henry
Archer, Jno. R.
Bennett, Edmund
Blake, Francis
Bourner, Jno.
Brandt, Alex.
Bressner, Jno.
Brown, Chas. A.
Clifton, Lewis R.
Connolly, Edward
Davis, Howard I.
Dennis, Jas.
Donohue, Thos.
Durham, Jas.
Edelin, Alex. W.
Elliott, Jos. W.
Ennis, Thos.
Essender, Wm.
Fiege, Chas.
Fillis, Edward
Ford, Clement

Goodman, Julius D.
Griffith, Edward
Hanna, Geo.
Harper, Lloyd
Herster, Fred'k
Hogan, Thos.
Holland, Thos. R.
Johnston, Jno. J.
Johnston, Jno. R.
Lawn, Edward
Leddard, Bernard
Leonard, Chas. H.
Lockington, Jas. A.
McCabe, Luke
McGinnis, Jas.
McNamee, Jas.
Melvin, Geo.
Miller, Wm.
Motter, Jno.
Mulhare, Bernard
Merritt, Sam'l

Pearce, Jno.
Parsons, Jas.
Rhodes, Geo.
Riley, Jno.
Roberts, Edward L.
Ruark, Michael
Sandler, Wm.
Schaeffer, Henry
Schaeffer, Benjamin
Shannon, Michael
Sherrington, Henry W.
Simonds, Albert
Stanton, Wm.
Tourney, Sylvester
Valiant, Geo. E. W.
Webber, Edward
Wellmore, Edward
Welsh, Martin
Welsh, Edward
Woods, Chas.
Wrea, Jno.

Co. F.

J. Louis Smith, Capt.
Wm. D. Hough, 1st Lieut.
Wm. J. Broadfoot, 2nd Lieut.
Joseph H. Stewart, 2nd Lieut.
Geo. W. Foos, 1st Sergt.
Jno. Marny, Sergt.
Jno. Morris, Sergt.

Sam'l A. Kennedy, Sergt.
Jno. Ryan, Corp.
Michael McCourt, Corp.
Edward Sheehan, Corp.
Owen Callen, Corp.
Francis Farr, Musician.

PRIVATES.

Angel, Thos.
Allen, Jas.
Brandt, Wm.
Behrnes, Barney,
Becknell, Fred'k
Beyer, Adam,
Blake, Jno.
Carr, Thos.
Chapin, Chas.
Condell, Sam'l
Conolly, Wm.
Cunningham, R.
Cummins, Daniel
Dougherty, Cornelius
Durst, Jno.
Eisenberger, Geo.
Eveline, Jno.
Gavin, Thos.
Golden, Jno.
Girvin, Jno.
Glossner, Hanas
Graham, Jesse
Graham, Geo. H.

Hagan, Jno.
Hamilton, Jacob
Hanna, Jno.
Hoffman, Geo.
Hunter, Jno.
Hutchinson, Thos.
Hartz, David
Inglehart, Edward
Kenney, Patrick
Knapp, Henry
Lusby, Jas.
Logue, Jno.
Logue, Michael
MacCubbin, R. W. Jr.
Marcus, Jas. T.
Mills, Wm. P.
Mihon, Martin
McCarthy, Daniel
McCevitt, Arthur
McCormick, Jno.
McClutchy, Jno.
McDermott, Jas.
McDonald, Patrick

McManus, Jas.
McMahon, Jas.
Magness, Wm.
McNally, Felix
Nolan, Jas.
Quin, Michael
Quin, Wm.
Ryan, Joseph
Rush, Peter
Rudden, Thos.
Sheedy, Daniel
Smith, Wm. A.
Smith, Thos.
Swan, Jas.
Swan, Geo. W.
Sweeting, Benj. F.
Thomas, Holbrook
Voght, F. E.
Warden, Wm.
Weitzell, Wm.
Wilson, Jno.
Woodward, Columbus
Weddinger, Ferdinand

Co. G.

Wilson C. Nicholas, Capt.
Alexander Cross, 1st Lieut.
Edward Deppish, 2nd Lieut.
Jno. J. Platt, 1st Sergt.
James Farrell, Sergt.
Louis Neidhammer, Sergt.

James Shields, Sergt.
George Ross, Corp.
Eli Fishpan, Corp.
Samuel Kirk, Corp.
Charles Fercoit, Corp.
Andrew Myers, Musician.

PRIVATES

Blunt, Robert
Brashears, Benton T.
Brady, Michael
Byers, William
Cantwell, Michael
Coombs, Charles
Dawson, Jno.
Deppish, Frank
Doyle, Jno.
Dyser, Louis
Eckhart, Charles
Eagger, Henry
Farrell, Wm.
Forrest, Zachariah
Fink, Henry

Goodwin, Jno.
Gordon, John H.
Gesdon, Walter
Griffith, Jno. Jas.
Griffith, Greenberry
Green, Charles
Greenfield, Wm.
Hanley, Thomas
Halpin, Thomas
Hartley, Wm. B.
Henderson, George
Hempston, Alex. T.
Hughes, Patrick,
Hutchinson, Joseph
Hood, George

Isaacs, William
Keyser, Herman
King, Jno.
Leonard, Michael
Logsden, Jno.
Lowrey, James
Martin, Wm. P.
Maloney, Wm.
Morris, Harry
Morris, George
Malden, Elias
Murphy, Jno.
Murphy, Dennis
Patrick, Jas. Thos.
Phillips, Jas. C.

Pigione, Joseph
Pilker, Michael
Quinn, Jno.
Raday, Patrick
Rhodes, Wm. Lee
Ryan, James

Ryan, Joseph
Reed, Samuel
Sahin, Joseph
Scholl, Charles
Simpson, H. A.
Simpson, Edward

Stewart, Henry
Strible, George
Sheehan, William
Sanders, Jas. H.
Suit, Michael
Wagner, Jno. G.

Co. H.

William H. Murray, Capt.
George Thomas, 1st Lieut.
Francis X. Ward, 2d Lieut.
Richard T. Gilmor, 2d Lieut.
Jno. H. Sullivan, 1st Sergt.
McHenry, Howard, Sergt.

James Lyon, Sergt.
Chapman B. Briscoe, Sergt.
Edward Johnson, Corp.
Richard C. Mackall, Corp.
Clapham Murray, Corp.
Wm. S. Lemmon, Corp.

PRIVATES.

Blackistone, Geo. W.
Bolling, Jno. M.
Bond, Jno. J.
Briscoe, David S.
Briscoe, Henry
Brogden, Sellman
Burke, John M.
Blackistone, Wm. T.
Carr, Wilson C. N.
Coakeley, Philip A.
Colston, Wm. E.
Coode, Demetrius
Cook, George R.
Costigan, Dorsey T.
Davies, Wm. H.
Davis, James A.
Denton, George
Dorsey, Ezekiel S.
Dorsey, Richard B.
Douglass, Jackson
Farr, Joseph R.
Gardiner, Wm. F.
Gill, John,
Gist, Washington I.
Grayson, Jas. B.
Greenwell, Thos. W. H.
Grogan, Chas. E.
Goldsmith, Jno. W.
Gwynn, Jas. J.
Hance, Jas. J.

Hebb, Henry J.
Hebb, Thos. A.
Harris, Wm. E.
Hoblitzell, Fetter S.
Hollyday, Wm. H.
Hough, Gresham,
Inloes, Chas. E.
Laird, Jas. W.
Laird, Wm. H.
Law, J. G. D.
Lemmon, George
Lemmon, Jno. S.
Levering, Thos. H.
Mackall, Thos. B.
Markoe, Frank
Marriott, Henry
McKim, W. Duncan,
McKim, Randolph H.
Monmonier, Jno. N. K.
Perry, Wm. T.
Peters, Winfield
Phillips, Jno. J.
Pinkney, Wm. S.
Pitts, Fred'k L.
Post, Jno. E. H.
Purnell, Wm.
Pinkney, Campbell W.
Price
Redmond, George
Rives, Francis S.

Rogers, Samuel B.
Russell, Elisha T.
Russell, Thos. A.
Ryan, Jas. A.
Ryce, Francis W.
Schley, Lake R.
Schliephake, Henry T.
Shanks, Daniel,
Sindall, Saml. W.
Smith, Wm. F.
Sollers, Summerville
Sothron, Webster H.
Thomas, Edwin
Thomas, Jno. H.
Thomas, Jas. W.
Tippett, Jas. B.
Tongue, James
Turner, Duncan M.
Valliant, Thos. R.
Watkins, Nich. I.
West, Edward L.
White, Jas. McK.
Williams, Aug. A.
Williams, Jno. P.
Williamson, George
Wise, Chas. B.
Wright, Daniel G.
West, Charles
Yellott, Washington,
Zollinger, William P.

Co. I.

Michael S. Robertson, Capt.
Hugh Mitchell, 1st Lieut.
Hezekiah H. Bean, 2d Lieut.
Eugene Diggs, 2d Lieut.
Jno. J. Brawner, 1st Sergt.
Jno. H. Stone, Sergt.

Wm. H. Rison, Sergt.
Warren W. Ward, Sergt.
Z. Francis Freeman, Corp.
Francis L. Higdon, Corp.
Thos. I. Green, Corp.
Thos. L. Hannon, Corp.

PRIVATES.

Adams, Franklin	Davis, Wm. F.	Mudd, Edwin C.
Adams, Jno. S.	Dent, George H.	Nicholson, Franklin T.
Bailey, Henry M.	Dooley, Robert	Page, Chas. C.
Beall, Wm. B.	Ferrall, Jno A.	Randle, Walter I.
Bivin, Zachariah	Ferguson, Jno.	Ransle, Andrew
Bivin, Wm. B.	Freeman, Philip	Richard, George
Bruce, William	Freeman, Thos. S.	Selby, John
Burttes, Chas. H.	Groves, Thos. F.	Shierbon, Wm.
Burttes, Thos. W.	Hammett, Jno. M.	Shorter, Thomas O.
Briscoe, Marshall	Herbert, Jno. P.	Simmes, Henry M.
Briscoe, Girard	Herbert, William	Swan, John
Barber, Jno. G.	Howard, Roberts	Sanders, Joseph
Ball, Dyonisius	Hayden, Charles G.	Sollers, Jas. H.
Cissell, Jas. T.	Hanson, Jno. D.	Sothron, Marshall
Clark, Jno. E.	Jenkins, Jno. E.	Taylor, George
Clements, Francis	Jamison, Francis	Thompson, Thomas M.
Chapalin, George	Klemkivitz, Benj.	Ward, William
Corry, Henry	Lacy, James A.	Webster, George
Dement, Benj. F.	Lacy, Robert	Webster, Wm.
Dement, Jno. H.	Leigh, Wm. G.	Wilson, Algernon
Downing, Jno. Z.	Lancaster, Sam'l	Wood, Henry W.
Dorsett, Jas. A.	Marceron, Albert	Wheatly, Wm. F.

Co. C. (Second)

Edmund Barry, Capt.	Albert Tolson, 1st Sergt.
John Marshall, 1st Lieut.	Richard Brown, Sergt.
Wm. H. Edelin, 2nd Lieut.	William Barry, Sergt.
Tom Washington Smith, 2nd Lieut.	

This Company was enlisted in Richmond and united with the Regiment but a few days prior to the movement from the valley to the right of McClellan's army at Richmond in June, 1862—After the seven days fight the Regiment was sent to Charlottesville, Va., and in August, 1862, was mustered out of the service at Gordonsville, Va. No muster roll of this Company has been found in the War records.

Battles and actions in which the 1st Maryland Infantry were engaged: Manassas, Mason's Hill, Munson's Hill, Rappahannock River, Front Royal, Winchester, Harrisonburg, Cross Keys, Mechanicsville, Gaines' Mill, Despatch Station, Malvern Hill, Harrison Landing.

COMPLIMENTARY ORDERS TO THE REGIMENT DURING THEIR SERVICE.

Headquarters, Winchester, June 22, 1861.

SPECIAL ORDER:

The Commanding General thanks Lieut. Col. Steuart and the Maryland Regiment for the faithful and exact manner in which they carried out his orders of the 19th inst. at Harper's Ferry. He is glad to learn that owing to their discipline, no private property was injured and no unoffending citizen disturbed. The Soldierly qualities of the Maryland Regiment will not be forgotten in the day of action.

By Order of

GENL. JOSEPH E. JOHNSTON.

May 22, 1862.

Col. Johnson will move the First Maryland to the *front* with all dispatch, and in conjunction with Wheats' Batallion attack the Enemy at Front Royal, the army will halt until you pass.

JACKSON.

From Genl. Ewell's Official Report of the Valley Campaign.

The history of the Maryland Regiment gallantly commanded by Col. Bradley T. Johnson during the Campaign of the Valley, would be the history of every action from Front Royal to Cross Keys. On the 6th, near Harrisonburg, the 58th Va. Reg. was engaged with the Pennsylvania Bucktails, the fighting being close and bloody, Col. Johnson came up with his Regiment in the hottest period, and by a dashing charge in flank drove the enemy off with heavy loss, capturing Lieut. Col. Kane commanding. In commemoration of this gallant conduct, I ordered one of the captured Bucktails to be appended as a trophy to their flag. The action is worthy of acknowledgement from a higher source more particularly as they avenged the death of the gallant Genl. Ashby who fell at the same time. Four color bearers were shot down in succession, but each time the Colors were caught before reaching the ground, and were finally borne by Corporal Daniel Shanks to the close of the action. On the 8th inst., at Cross Keys, they were opposed to three of the enemy's Regiments in succession.

Genl. Stonewall Jackson's report of the Valley Campaign says:

Apprehending that the Federals would make a more serious attack, Ashby called for an Infantry support, the Brigade of Genl. Geo. H. Steuart was accordingly ordered forward, in a short time the 58th Va. became engaged with a Pennsylvania Regiment called the Bucktails, when Col. Johnson of the First Maryland Regiment coming up in the hottest period of the fire, charged gallantly into its flank, and drove the enemy with heavy loss from the field, capturing Lieut. Col. Kane commanding. In this skirmish our infantry loss was seventeen killed, fifty wounded and three missing, in this affair Genl. Turner Ashby was killed.

HEADQUARTERS THIRD DIVISION.

GENERAL ORDER NO. 30.

In commemoration of the gallant conduct of the First Maryland Regiment, on the 6th of June, when led by Col. Bradley T. Johnson, they drove back with loss the Pennsylvania Bucktail Rifles, in the engagement near Harrisonburg, Rockingham Co., Va. Authority is given to have one of the captured Bucktails, the insignia of the Federal Regiment appended to the Color Staff of the First Maryland Regiment.

By Order of,

MAJOR GENERAL EWELL,
JAMES BARBOUR, A. A. G.

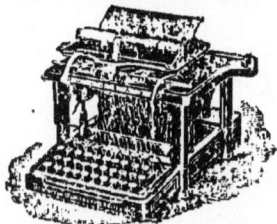

SECOND MARYLAND INFANTRY.

FIELD AND STAFF.

LIEUTENANT-COLONEL,
 JAMES R. HERBERT.

MAJOR,
 WM. W. GOLDSBOROUGH.

SURGEON,
 RICHARD P. JOHNSON.

ASST. SURGEON,
 DeWILTON SNOWDEN.

A. Q. M.,
 JOHN E. HOWARD.

ADJUTANT,
 J. WINDER LAIRD.

SERGEANT-MAJOR,
 WM. R. McCULLOUGH.

Q. M. SERGEANT,
 EDWIN JAMES.

ORDNANCE SERGEANT,
 FRANCIS L. HIGDON.

CHIEF MUSICIAN,
 MICHAEL A. QUINN.

Co. A,

Wm. H. Murray, 1st Capt.
Geo. Thomas, Capt.
Clapham Murray, 1st Lieut.
Wm. P. Zollinger, 2nd Lieut.
Wm. I. Blackiston, 1st Sergt.
Jas. F. Pearson, Sergt.
Jas. W. Thomas, Sergt.

Ezekiel S. Dorsey, Sergt.
Wm. H. Smith, Sergt.
Willis Brancock, Corp.
Chas. E. Maguire, Corp.
George Denton, Corp.
Lawrence K. Thomas, Corp.
Wm. Gannon, Musician.

PRIVATES.

Adair, Wm. R.
Bailey, Wm. T.
Barry, Philip.
Bond, Benj. F.
Bond, Jno.
Bowdoin, Lloyd
Bowling, Chas. F.
Bowling, Thos. B.
Bowling, Wallace
Braddock, Chas. S.
Bryan, Edmund
Baxley, Wm. G. D.
Bruce, Wm.
Bowly, W. H.
Burch, Jno. H.
Clayville, Moses
Carey, Jas. E.
Chandler, W. S. J.
Davis, Geo. W.
Davis, Jacob N.
Deale, Theophilus N.
Durner, Jno. F.
Edelin, Wm. J.
Emory, Albert T.
Feige, Chas. L.
Fitzgerald, Jno. E.
Freeman, Bernard

Fulton, Alexander
Gallagher, Howard L.
Gardner, Wm. F.
Gill, Summerville P.
Glenn, Sam'l T.
Goodwin, Jno.
Grammer, Fred'k L.
Grayson, Spence M.
Grogan, Jas. J.
Hammett, Jno. T.
Hance, Wm. H.
Hanson, Notley
Harrison, Thos. D.
Harrison, W. H.
Henry, Jno. C.
Herster, Fred'k
Hoffman, Wm. H.
Hollyday, Henry
Hollyday, Lamar
Hollyday, Wm. H.
Hopkins, Sam'l J.
Howard, David R.
Hubball, Bernard
Hunter, Jno. I.
Hughes, Alexander
Hubbard, Wm. L.
Heenan, N.

Hardesty, Jno. W.
Iglehart, I. Jas.
Ives, Leonard W.
Jennings, Benj. R.
Joy, Jos. I.
James, Edwin
Klinkiewicz, Thaddeus A.
Kennedy, Arthur
Laird, W. H.
Loane, Wm. T. J.
Lowe, Wm. E.
Lowe, Wrighton L.
Luchesi, David H.
Lake, Craig
Lloyd, T. Chas.
Lake, Jno. C.
Marden, Geo. M.
Marney, Jno.
McCevitt, Arthur
McCormick, Lewis D.
McCourt, Michael
McIntyre, G. W.
McCormick, H. A.
Morrison, Wilbur
McDaniel, Jno. W.
McDonald, Patrick
Miller, Andrew T.

Murray, Alexander
Nicolai, Herman
Owens, Henry C.
O'Brien, Thos.
O'Donovan, Edward
Pace, David P.
Phelps, Jas. J.
Peregoy, Jas. A.
Peters, Thos.
Porter, Wm. J.
Prentiss, Wm. S.
Phyfer, Henry

Pratt, Thos. St.George
Pindall, Philip
Raley, Jas. S.
Shanley, Thos. E.
Smith, H. Tillard
Sollers, Andrew J.
Sollers, Sommerville
Steele, Chas. H.
Starlings, Geo. C.
Sanderson, Frank H.
Taylor, Geo. L.
Thelin, Wm. T.

Tilghman, Rich'd C.
Trego, Jno. L.
Toy, Jos. L.
Trail, Chas. M.
Trippe, Andrew C.
Wagner, Jno. G.
Weems, Chas. H.
Williams, Jno. P.
Windoph, Jno. H.
Wilson, Jno.
White, Jas. McKenny
Zollinger, Jacob C.

Co. B.

J. Parran Crane, Capt.
J. H. Stone, 1st Lieut.
Chas. B. Wise, 2nd Lieut.
Jas. H. Wilson, 2nd Lieut.
Philip T. Reeder, 1st Sergt.
Jno. G. Barber, Sergt.
Francis Z. Freeman, Sergt.

Wittingham Hammett, Sergt.
Thos. Simms, Corp.
Wm. F. Wheatley, Corp.
Jno. Z. Downing, Corp.
Albert Fenwick, Corp.
Chas. T. Drury, Musician.

PRIVATES.

Alvey, Jas. P.
Artis, Jeremiah
Ball, Dionysius
Bailey, Jas. T.
Beale, Rob't
Browne, Gustavus
Bond, Jas. O.
Ching, Garrett
Chinn, Jno. H.
Clark, Jno. E.
Clark, Wm. A.
Combs, Edgar
Corry, Jas. B.
Corry, Henry
Dent, Clay H.
Delozier, Geo.
Delozier, Thos. J.
Delozier, Jno.
Duke, Jno. F.
Drury, Wm. C.
Evans, Dallas J.

Foxwell, Chas. J.
Ford, Henry
Freeman, Marion
Freeman, Thos. S.
Grove, Thos. F.
Herbert, Wm.
Herbert, Jas. R.
Hazell, Patrick
Hayden, Geo.
Hayden, Jno. A.
Jenkins, Jas. E.
Junger, Jno. H.
Joy, J. E.
Keech, Jas. H.
Lambson, Jas. B.
Long, Jeff T.
MaGill, Thos. F.
Matthews, Wm. G.
Mills, Jno. C.
Milstead, Jos. H.
Moran, Rinaldo J.

McLeod, Harry C.
Moore, Warren F.
Neal, Augustine
Page, Wm.
Page, Washington
Parsons, Jas. T.
Penn, Jno. T.
Paigo, C. Craig
Robertson, G. H.
Semmes, Lewis S.
Semmes, H. F.
Smith, Peter P.
Simms, W. H.
Tennison, Bernard Z.
Turner, Wm. L.
Turner, Henry
Wills, Jno. W.
Wills, Jas. A.
Wise, Henry A.
Wood, Walter
Wheatley, Wm. F.
Webster, Jas. R.

Co. C.

Ferdinaud Duvall, Capt.
Chas. W. Hodges, 1st Lieut.
Thos. C. Tolson, 2nd Lieut.
Jos. W. Barber, 2nd Lieut.
Wm. T. Outten, 1st Sergt.
Rob't T. Hodges, Sergt.
Geo. Probest, Sergt.

Wm. Ritter, Sergt.
Thos. D. Barron, Sergt.
Edward A. Welch, Corp.
Beale D. Mullikin, Corp.
Jno. W. Collins, Corp.
Chas. Clayton, Corp.

PRIVATES.

Anderson, Rich'd T.
Anderson, Sam'l
Blumenauer, Jno. M.
Clagett, Wm. H.
Cooksey, Theo.
Clough, Rob't H.
Crawford, Henry H.
Cushing, Rob't H.
Castle, Jas. L.
Duvall, Daniel
Duvall, Tobias
Duvall, Evans
Duvall, Franklin
Dawson, Rob't M.
Dorsey, Jas. E.
Duvall, Sam'l
Davis, Michael
Dulaney, Jeremiah
Ellis, Jno. T.
Edgar, Thos.
Ford, Clement S.
Grace, Wm.
Gibson, Wm. C.
Garrison, Rob't D.

Hamilton, Sam'l H.
Hardcastle, Wm. R.
Herbert, Chas. F.
Hood, Jno. M.
Hammond, Chas.
Haller, Jno. E.
Hamilton, Beale D.
Hammond, Edgar
Judge, Edward S.
Jones, Jno. T.
Loughton, Henry
Lane, Wm. B.
Lanahan, Benj. L.
Lawson, Jas. A.
Miller, Jno. C.
Mackabee, W. S.
Mackabee, Rich'd T.
Mitchell, Thos. L.
Mulliken, Walter
Michael, Jno.
McGena, Jno.
Moog, Jas. R.
McCann, W. D.
McWilliams, Jas.

Nash, Jas.
Nichols, W. L.
Onion, Rich'd T.
Orr, Peter
O'Byrn, Jno. T.
Payne, Benj.
Roberts, Geo.
Steele, Frank K.
Storm, Francis E.
Skinner, Wm. A.
Shipley, Wm. H.
Schultz, Justus
Twilley, Geo. H.
Tolson, Frank A.
Valiant, Ed. S.
Veit, Lewis H.
Welch, Rob't H.
White, Jno. G.
Wentworth, Geo. W.
Wheatley, Frank M.
Watts, Joshua
Watts, Jno.
Willis, Rob't W.

Co. D.

Jas. L. McAleer, Capt.
Jas. S. Franklin, 1st Lieut.
Sam'l T. McCullough, 2nd Lieut.
Thos. C. Butler, 1st Sergt.
Wm. Jenkins, Sergt.
J. Wm. Proudt, Sergt.

Isaac Sherwood, Sergt.
Edwin Gover, Sergt.
Geo. W. McAtee, Corp.
Alfred Riddlemoser, Corp.
Jno. McCready, Corp.

PRIVATES.

Brown, Jas. A.
Chilcot, Joshua
Crummer, Armstrong
Davis, Geo. W.
Dode, Sam'l
Devries, Jno.
Goldsborough, N. Lee
Green, Lewis
Hammett, David
Harney, Daniel
Hogarthy, Wm.
Harley, Job

Hays, Jno.
Hurley, Jno.
Hines, Thos. J.
Johnson, Jno.
Jones, Geo. W.
Kane, Bernard
Killman, Rich'd
Kerns, Cornelius
Lamb, Jno.
Leich, Christopher C.
Lipscomb, Philip
Lynch, Jno.

McAtee, Henry
McCready, Thos. D.
Owens, W. Beall
Owings, Joshua
Phillips, Abraham
Riddlemoser, David
Septer, Jno. H.
Shephard, Rich'd H.
Spence, Jno.
Watts, Wm.
Webb, Emmett M.

Co. E.

John W. Torsch, Capt.
Wm. J. Broadfoot, 1st Lieut.
Wm. R. Byus, 2d Lieut.
Jos. P. Quinn, 2d Lieut.
Samuel Kirk, 1st Sergt.
Geo. L. Ross, Sergt.
Wilbur Rutter, Sergt.

Wm. Heaphy, Sergt.
John Cain, Corp.
Lewis P. Staylor, Corp.
Jas. Reddie, Corp.
Benj. F. Amos, Corp.
Joseph Smith, Musician.
Jas. L. Aubrey, Musician.

PRIVATES.

Applegarth Jas. B.
Barry, Michael
Byns, Chas. C.
Byns, Stanley M.
Brown, John
Brandt, William
Brandt, Alex
Burke, Michael
Butler, Elisha
Cartwell, Jas.
Clarke, Joseph
Dawson, Robert A.
Dawson, Levin G.
Fallon, James
Fallis, Edward
Gavin, Wm.
Gibbons, John

Grant, John
Hebling, Stephen
Hanley, James
Hagley, Alphonsus
Koppleman, John
Lyons, Wm. H.
Lemates, Jas.
Lawn, Edward
Lee, William C.
Murray, John
Moore, Augustus,
Miller, Jacob
McLaughlin, Thomas
Martin, John N.
Moran, Wm. P.
McMahan, Frank
Moore, P. M.

McGee, Daniel
Mynch, Christopher
Noonan, Michael
O'Hallin, Martin
Rush, Peter
Roberts, Frank
Rutter, Elisha
Ridgel, James
Radecke, H. H.
Stansbury, Jno. L.
Sheehan, Edward
Shields, Owens
Sheedy, Daniel
Sullivan, John
Unkles, Wm. F.
Wilkinson, Wm. A.

Co. F.

A. J. Gwynn, Capt.
Jno. W. Polk, 1st Lieut.
David C. Forrest, 2d Lieut.
Jno. G. Hyland, 2d Lieut.
Nicholas J. Mills, 1st Sergt.
Walter J. Randall, Sergt.

Philip T. Muirhead, Sergt.
Thos. O. Hodges, Sergt.
Joseph Wagner, Sergt.
Jas. H. Dixon, Corp.
Jas. T. Brown, Corp.
Washington Martin, Corp.

PRIVATES.

Atzrodt, Henry
Anderson, Leroy
Boswell, Josiah T.
Briscoe, Marshall
Brawner, Wm. F.
Brook, Jno. P.
Clement, Francis
Clagett, Geo. H.
Clagett, Edward L.
Clagett, Jno. W.
Cretin, Andrew L.
Cretin, Henry
Cretin, Hillary
Dement, Benj. F.
Dement, Wm. S.
Dooley, Bernard
Dunnington, Lemuel

Doyle, Philip
Gray, Joseph
Gardner, James
Guy, Geo. W.
Green, Jno. T.
Hodges, Benj.
Hearne, Wm. H.
Huffington, Jno.
Hubbard, Jno. L.
Hurley, Abel
Hoye, Chas. A.
Holden, Robert
Keepers, Alexis
Knott, M. T.
Kennerly, Wm. R.
Mewshaw, Ebenezer

Martin, Joseph
Obendoffer, Augustus
Opper, Conrad
Polk, Samuel
Sollers, Jas. H.
Smith, Wm. S.
Thompson, Jno. E.
Taylor, Henry G.
Thompson, John W.
Wade, Chas. E.
Wade, Geo. A.
Webb, Thos. J.
Wilcombe, Caspar
Wright, Joel D.
Woodford, Arthur
Wagner, R.

Co. G.

Thos. R. Stewart, Capt.
G. G. Gwillette, 1st Lieut.
Geo. Brighthaupt, 2nd Lieut.
Wm. C. Wrightson, 2nd Lieut.
Dan'l A. Fenton, 1st Sergt.
Geo. W. Manning, Sergt.
Michael C. Holohan, Sergt.

Patrick O'Connell, Sergt.
Henry Algernon, Sergt.
Jas. E. Briddle, Corp.
Henry A. Mumford, Corp.
Wm. Lord, Corp.
Benj. F. Twilley, Corp.

PRIVATES.

Abbott, Jas.
Atkins, S. E.
Brannock, Thos. H.
Bowen, Henry
Brannock, Wm. J.
Boyles, Daniel
Breslin, E. W.
Callahan, Jno.
Clarke, Chas. A.
Cator, Wm. B.
Calhoun, Wm. H.
Duvall, Jno. H.
Davis, Jno. S.
Edelin, Francis D.
Etchison, Wm. L.
Elligett, Michael
Eagan, Peter
Edelin, Jno. D.
Freeland, Thos. E.

Fentswait, J. R.
Fountain, W. B.
Gosson, J. H.
Hutchinson, Jno. T.
Hopkins, Henry H.
Henderson, Wm. W.
Henderson, Peter
Hutchins, Joseph
Hines, Michael
Heck, Rob't
Heck, Jacob
Langford, Geo. W.
Lannahan, Daniel
Littleford, J. S.
Manly, Joseph
Mumford, Wm. R.
Mayberry, J. P.
Messick, Ross
Pickel, Wm.

Furnell, Jno. J.
Paul, Wm. J.
Robey, Wm. H.
Rider, Martin L.
Reed, Wm. T.
Robbins, Wm.
Scoggins, Daniel
Thompson, Jno. W.
Vickers, Washington A.
Waters, Jno. W.
Waters, Jesse
Wingate, Fred'k A.
Williamson, P. B.
Weaver, Lewis H.
Wheatley, Levin
Woolford, S. L.
Yingle, A. B. P.

Co. H.

J. Thos. Bussey, Capt.
Thos. O'Brien, 1st Sergt.
Jno. J. Powers, Sergt.

Patrick Keenan, Corp.
Jno. J. Ward, Corp.

PRIVATES.

Adams, J. Q.
Brown, Jas.
Booth, Jno.
Bush, Wm.
Cavanaugh, Francis C.
Carroll, Jas.
Carlin, Lawrence
Collins, Chas.
Carroll, Lawrence
Collins, Richard
Clark, Jas.
Christy, Wm.
DeGrey, Lewis F.
Donohue, Jno
Driscoll, Jas.

Eagan, Thos. T.
Flannigan, Jno.
Flood, Peter
Graham, Thos.
Gevin, Peter M.
Gardiner, Benj.
Hargey, Wm.
Holloway, Michael
Hays, J. G.
Kelley, Jas.
Kelley, Jno. L.
Kelley, Jno.
Morgan, Wm.
Murphy, Jno.
Martin, Jno.

Murray, Wm.
McKea, Jno.
Nichols, Jno.
Needham, Geo.
O'Brien, Jas.
Parker, Jno.
Powers, Jno.
Ryan, Jno.
Robinson, Jas.
Shetkins, Jno.
Stephens, Jno.
Ward, Maurice
Welch, Edward
Walsh, Edward
Wagner, J. J.

Battles in which the Second Maryland Regiment Infantry were engaged: Winchester, Gettysburg, Cold Harbor, White Oak Swamp, Weldon Rail Road, Squirrel Level Road, Hatchers Run, Pegrams Farm, Appomattox, Petersburg.

Steuart's brigade to which the 2nd Maryland was assigned, assaulted Culps' Hill at Gettysburg, July 2nd, 1863, and took the line of Federal works, occupy-the same through the night. On the following morning a further advance movement was attempted, which however failed, and after a desperate conflict the Confederate line was retired to the position on Rock Creek. The 2nd Maryland have commemorated this service by the erection of a monument which stands on the Federal line of works. The regiment carried into action about 400 muskets, of which force more than one half were killed or wounded.

From the *Richmond Sentinel.*

June 6th, 1864.

The public have already been informed, through the columns of the public journals, of the general results of the late engagements between the forces of General Lee and General Grant. But they have not yet, learned the particulars, which are always most interesting, and in some instances, owing to the confusion which generally attends large battles, they have been misinformed on some points. It is now known by the public that the enemy were momentarily successful in one of their assaults on the lines held by Major General Breckinridge's division, which might have resulted in disaster to our cause. It will be interesting to all to know what turned disaster into victory, and converted a triumphant column into a flying rabble. The successful assault of the enemy was made under cover of darkness, before the morning star had been hid by the light of the sun. They came gallantly forward in spite of a severe fire from General Echols' brigade, and in spite of the loss of many of their men, who fell like autumn leaves, until the ground was almost blue and red with their uniforms and their blood. They rushed in heavy mass over our breastworks. Our men, confused by the suddenness of the charge and borne down by the rush of the enemy, retreated, and all now seemed to be lost. At this junction the Second Maryland Infantry, of Col. Bradley T. Johnson's command, now in charge of Captain J. P. Crane, were roused from their sleep. Springing to their arms they formed in a moment, and rushing gallantly forward, poured a deadly fire into the enemy, and then charged bayonet. The enemy were, in turn, surprised at the suddenness and vim of this assault. They gave back—they became confused; and General Finnegan's forces coming up, they took flight; but not until nearly a hundred men were stretched on the plain, from the fire of the Second Maryland Infantry, and many others captured. Lieutenant Charles B. Wise of Company B, now took possession of the guns, which had been abandoned by our forces, and with the assistance of some of his own men and some of General Finnegan's command, poured a deadly fire into the retreating column of the enemy. Thus was the tide of battle turned, and this disaster converted into a success. I am informed that the whole force of the enemy which came within our lines would have been captured, had it not been for the mistake of an officer who took the enemy for our own men, and thus checked for a few moments the charge of the Second Maryland Infantry. I take pleasure in narrating these deeds of our Maryland brethren and doubt not you will join in the feeling.—

General Lee referring to the behavior of the 2nd Maryland on the above occasion, speaks of them as the "gallant battalion."

FIRST MARYLAND CAVALRY.

FIELD AND STAFF.

LIEUT.-COLONELS.

RIDGELY BROWN. ROBERT CARTER SMITH. GUS. W. DORSEY.

MAJORS.

RIDGELY BROWN. ROBERT CARTER SMITH.

ADJUTANTS.

GEO. W. BOOTH. JNO. E. H. POST.

ASSIST. SURGEON.

WILBUR R. McKNEW.

A. Q. M.

IGNATIUS W. DORSEY.

SERGT. MAJORS.

EDWARD JOHNSON. JOHN E. H. POST. ARTHUR BOND.

Q. M. SERGEANT.

CHAS. J. WEGNER.

ORD. SERGEANT.

EDWARD JOHNSON.

Co. A.

Frank A. Bond, Capt.
Thomas Griffith, 1st Lieut.
J. A. V. Pue, 2d Lieut.
Edward Beatty, 2d Lieut.
Jno. H. Scholl, 1st Sergt.
Hammond Dorsey, Sergt.
Frank Griffith, Sergt.

Joshua Riggs, Sergt.
Chas. R. Cockey, Sergt.
Wm. Wilson, Corp.
Bazil Clark, Corp.
Arthur Bond, Corp.
John Harding.

PRIVATES.

Artis, Jeremiah
Armstrong, Joshua
Bracco, Edward
Brown, John R.
Beckett, John M.
Bender, Frank
Bell, Henry
Boyd, Andrew
Bond, Saml. G.
Bond, W. W.
Bond, H.
Brown, C. C.
Clarke, David
Clarke, John
Clarke, William
Carter, R. W.
Cockey, Sprigg
Canby, Benj.

Childs, W. H.
Childs, Soper
Covington, Jesse
Crane, Brent
Clagett, John
Crawford, Thomas
Carey, John B.
Cannon, J. G.
Dorsey, John
Dorsey, Pulaski
Dorsey, Andrew
Dorsey, Lloyd
Dorsey, Upton
Dorsey, Gustavus
Dorsey, C. W.
Dickerson, L. T.
Dunlop, Jos. I.
Durburrow, J. C.

Ditty, C. Irving,
Dorsey, Harry
Dorsey, J. Pembrook
Dorsey, I. G.
Edelin, Wm.
Foster, Michael
Forsyth, Henry
Ferguson, John
Griffith, David
Gill, John
Griffin, Geo. C.
Gephart, Solomon
Graham
Hall, Edward
Hannaway, Wm.
Henden, Thos.
Hough, Gresham
Hutton, Chas.

Hunter, Thos.
Harry, James
Heighe, John
Henderson, Gaither
Hammond, Chas.
Horner, Frank
Hough, Samuel
Harrison, C. H.
Johnson, Otis
Johnson, J. N.
Johnson, John
Jackson, Andrew J.
Jones, John
Johnson, Edward
Keene, Robt. G.
Kennedy, McPherson
Kettlewell, E. R.
Kenley, J. R.
Lechlider, George
Langley, Thos.
Linthicum, Edwin
Locker, Edward
Locker, Wm.
Leisher, G. W.
Leiter, Charles
Lincoln, Rush J.
Lipscomb, Frank

Murdoch, Augustus
Mooney, John
Magruder, Zach
Maynard, Thos.
McDowell, Chas.
Mason, R. R.
Miller, Wm.
Nelson, R. W.
Pue, Ferd C.
Price, M. A.
Polk, Truston
Pretzman, D. C.
Price, Kennedy
Patrick, Chas. R.
Polk, Saml.
Patrick, John
Perdue, John
Peddicord, S.
Porter, J. J.
Rico, Geo.
Riggs, Reuben
Ridgely, John
Rozier, Chas.
Richardson, Howard
Riley, Thos. S.
Sellman, John

Shipley, Saml.
Smith, Daniel
Stone, Henry,
Schwartz, Augustus
Slingluff, F. C.
Stone, C.
Scott, Geo.
Tolby, George
Treackle, Emmet
Thompson, Edward
Thompson, G. L.
Thompson, Dorsey
Tschiffely, Edgar L.
Webster, W. H.
Warring, Henry
Webb, Wm.
Worthington, Joshua
Warfield, A. G.
Wooten, Henry E..
Watkins, Lewis J.
Whalen, John W.
Wisner, Jno. D.
Worthington, Chas.
Warfield, G.
Woolford, A.
Zepp, Chas. P.

Co. B.

Geo. M. Emack, Capt.
Mason E. McKnew, 1st Lieut.
Adolphus Cook, 2nd Lieut.
Henry C. Blackiston, 2nd Lieut.
S. B. Spencer, 1st Sergt.
W. A. Wilson, Sergt.

W. H. W. Guyther, Sergt.
D. M. Turner, Sergt.
O. H. Perry, Sergt.
G. M. Serpell, Corp.
J. J. Spear, Corp.
Pembroke Jones, Corp.

PRIVATES.

Aisquith, Hobart
Baden, J. M.
Barry, W. D.
Beale, Alex.
Bean, Thos. L.
Bean, W. M.
Bond, J. W.
Bowling, Alex.
Bowling, Nicholas.
Boarman, J. N.
Blackiston, S. H.
Brent, Geo. T.
Bryan, W. L.
Burch, J. H.
Bullen, R. B.
Bradley, J.
Briscoe, P.
Crawford, H. V. B.
Cropper, Thos. E.
Cooper, W. T.
Davis, P. A.
Deakins, J. R. H.

Dix, Wm. T.
Dutton, S. S.
Dyer, A. M.
Earle, Jas. T.
Eareckson, F. G.
Embert, J. R. H.
Ebert, Chas.
Eckhart, Chas. H.
Elliott, G. M.
Elliott, J. T.
Ferrall, Thos.
Gibson, Jno. E.
Gough, Chas. E.
Green, W. O.
Hambleton, J. P.
Hill, J. P.
Hickey, J. F.
Hickey, E. P.
Hearne, Sam'l B.
Hucorn, Jno. F.
Hearne, B. G.
Jeffers, W. H.

Jones, Jno.
Key, Rich'd H.
Keets, Jno. F.
Lyons, Bunton
McCormick, B. H.
McLeod, W.
McCall, R.
Nailor, T. K.
Noel, E.
Perrio, Thos. H.
Price, Jas. H.
Parker, Geo. T.
Perkins, L. O.
Reed, Mingel
Smith, James
Seaggs, Edward O.
Spear, D. W. C.
Spear, Edwin W.
Stanley, Chas. H.
Stevers, James C.
Scaggs, J.
Strong, W.

Tolson, W. C.
Tolson, Chas. E.
Tunis, Theopholus
Tunis, Jno.
Thomas, Jno. E.
Thomas, Edwin

Tippett, M. A. K.
Waring, Jas.
Waring, Edwin
Wissman, L. O.
Wilks, Thos. M.
Williams, Jno. W.

Wooley, Geo.
Wright, R. B.
Willis, Thos.
Watkins, N. W.
Wilson, J. K.

Co. C.

Rob't C. Smith, Capt.
Geo. Howard, 1st Lieut.
T. Jeff Smith, 2nd Lieut.
T. J. Green, 2nd Lieut.
Graeme Turnbull, 2nd Lieut.
Jas. D. Walters, 2nd Lieut.
Illinois Caruthers, 1st Sergt.

Geo. Smith Norris, Sergt.
E. Clarence Neale, Sergt.
Wm. F. Dorsey, Sergt.
Hamilton Lefevre, Sergt.
Richard Knox, Corp.
Richard C. Smith, Corp.
Lafayette Hause, Corp.

PRIVATES.

Anderson, Oscar
Barber, Christopher
Barbour, Oscar
Brehm, Jno. P.
Billop, Christopher
Biays, Geo.
Brown, Rob't
Bull, Elijah
Bateman, H.
Barnes, Rich'd
Bowie, Harry
Byrne
Chisildine, W. C.
Cook, Geo.
Claude, Hammond
Cretin, Jno.
Crittenden, C.
Chambers, Rob't M.
Carey, Michael.
Crane, Wm.
Clements, Wm.
Dall, H. McP.
Dougherty, Jas.
Dittus, Jno. P.
Dance, E. Scott
Emory, Dan'l G.
Elder, Geo. H.
Elder, Lawrence
Edwards, Wm.
Foley, David R.
Flanegan, Jno.
Gill, Wm. H.
Gough, Chas. E.
Grogan, Rob't R.
Gray, Henry L.
Goodman, Otho
Giles, Wm. F.
Grove, Thos.
Glenn, Clement
Glenn, Elias
Glenn, Francis
George, Thomas
Grogan, J.
Graham, Jesse
Hayward, Henry

Hance, Jas. J.
Hartigan, Jno. J.
Hayward, Henry
Heimiller, Herman
Holbrook, Jno.
Howard, R. McG.
Howard, Carroll C.
Howard, Jno. E.
Herron, Geo.
Hollyday, Geo.
Hager, Jno.
Harry, Jno.
Hudgins, Chas.
Hume, J. R. F.
Harry, Albert
Inloes, Chas
Jones, Wm. O.
Jones, G. W.
Jenkins, Poland
Jenkins, Geo. C.
Krebs, Chas.
Kettlewell, Chas.
Kimball, H.
Lurman, Gustav W.
Lemmon, W. S.
Liambaugh, Wm. C.
Latrobe, R. Stewart
Lyon, Sam'l H.
Leazey, Jos. H.
Lumkin, Jas. T.
Levering, Thos. H.
McWilliams, Hugh
McBride, Thos. C.
McCourt, Jas. R.
McCleary, Peter H.
McKee, Jas.
Magill, Davidge
Magill, Wm. D.
Mitchell, Levin
Macatee, J. J.
Macatee, S. E.
Macatee, Henry
Makomer, Mathias
Makall, Leonard
Myers, Clinton

Neale, Wilford
Norris, Alex. Jr.
Oates, Jas. F.
Pool, Wm. C.
Pue, W. H.
Post, Jno. E. H.
Palmer, A.
Pue, Arthur
Riley, Jno. P.
Ridgely, Jno.
Rogers, Sam'l
Rogers, Jas. P.
Rogers, Philip
Rose, Porter E.
Reach, Jno.
Redwood, A. C.
Redwood, J. W.
Raphael, Eugene
Stonebraker, Jos. R.
Sanders, Hillen T.
Shroff, Peter F.
Spencer, Jervis
Stone, Jos.
Smith, Wilson C.
Sullivan, Frank
Slater, Wm. J.
Shorb, Donald M. M.
Snowden, Jno.
Street, Jas.
Shiplett, P.
Scott, J. E.
Tennant, T.
Thomas, Raleigh C.
Towles, J. C.
Valentine, Geo.
Williams, Aug. A.
Welch, Jos. C.
Wusten, Henry
Willis, Chas. W.
Wood, I. J.
Wharton, Wm. F.
Weber, Edward
Williams, Thos. P.
Wilde, Geo.
Young, Washington

Co. D.

Warner G. Welsh, Capt.
Wm. H Dorsey, 1st Lieut.
Stephen D. Lawrence, 2nd Lieut.
Milton Welsh, 2nd Lieut.
Phineas I. Davis, 1st Sergt.
Upton L. Dorsey, Sergt.
Thos. G. Worthington, Sergt.

Albert Jones, Sergt.
Lewis W. Trail, Sergt.
Geo. R. Simpson, Corp.
Edwin Selvage, Corp.
Geo. R. Cather, Corp.
Rich H. Norris, Corp.

PRIVATES.

Bromwell, Thos. C. S.
Bromwell, Henry H.
Bromwell, Josiah R.
Brasher, Thos P.
Butler, Cyrus S.
Boyle, Chas. B.
Baughman, L. Victor
Barrick, Wm.
Cole, Chas. N.
Carter, Grafton
Corcoran, Thos. W.
Clarke, Chas. H.
Clark, Joseph
Cleary, Vachel T.
Crisswell, Jno. O.
Chesler, Henry
Clagett, Rob't
Dale, Wm. F.
Delashmutt, Wm. H.
Davis, Evan
Davis, Thos. S.
Doomandy, Jno.
Ewing, Harvey S.
Ewing, Wm. F.
Ensor, Zadock
Ebbert,
Fearhake, Adolphus
Fitzgerald, Thos.
Flint, Joseph
Funk, Chas. D.
Grabill, Abraham W.
Grimes, Cornelius
Geasey, Jas. W.
Geasey, Chas. H.

Gibson, Henry
Grimes, Harry
Geiger, Jno.
Hammond, Denton
Hammond, Oliver B.
Hoyle, Nathan L.
Harrison, Wm.
Hergesheimer, David
Herring, Frank
Hillary, Thos.
Jones, Edward C.
Jones, Spencer C.
Kemp, Chas.
Kemp, Theodore
Knauff, Geo. W.
Launden, Chas.
Lickle, Jno. D.
McDaniel, Jno.
Mercer, Sam'l B.
Miles, Geo. T.
McLanahan, Wm. H.
Merryman, Joseph
Myers, Thos.
Maynard, Albert
MacKubbin, Jas. B.
McSherry, Edward L.
Matthews, H. H.
Maguire, Jos. E.
Neal, Frank
Neal, Harry
Obenderfe, Jno.
O'Leary, Jerry
Ott, Geo. W.
Price, Jas. E.

Pope, Wm. H.
Placide, Rob't
Raitt, Chas. H.
Radcliffe, Edward
Raborg, Christopher
Raborg, Wm.
Rosau, Chas. W.
Roley, Thos.
Shafer, Cornelius L.
Steres, Christopher
Simons, Albert
Stephenson, Thos. H.
Stephenson, Dawson
Shultz, William
Steele, Jno.
Sollers, Wm. O.
Snook, Jerome H.
Shafer, Thos. H.
Shower, Geo.
Sisson Christopher
Schessler, Henry
Taylor, Chas. J.
Tyler, Jno. B.
Tyler, Geo.
Tyler, Albert
Traphan, Joseph
Thomas, Wm.
Worthington, Geo. E.
Woodward, Columbus, O.
Weaver, Hiram,
Wilson, Frederick
Welsh, Luther
Wilson, Rob't
Warfield.

Co. E.

William I. Raisin, Capt.
S. B. Burroughs, 1st Lieut.
Nathaniel Chapman, 2nd Lieut.
Jos K. Roberts, Jr., 2nd Lieut.
Townley Robey, 1st Sergt.
Jno. Savage, Sergt.

Solomon Wright, Sergt.
Thos. H. Gemmill, Sergt.
Geo. T. Hollyday, Corp.
Benj. J. Turton, Corp.
Henry C. Wallis, Corp.
Jno. W. Slaven, Corp.

PRIVATES.

Booker, Wm. T.
Bourne, Jas. B.
Baden, Wm. A. H.
Brawner, T. M.
Brooke, Geo. W.
Brooke, Clements

Boone, W. C.
Bryant, Geo. H.
Bryan, W. C.
Baker, H. W.
Cox, Jas. B.
Connick, Rob't

Cockey, Jno. P.
Chesley, Dan'l S.
Cator, Benj.
Crawford, Geo. I.
Cadle, Jas. R.
Cleary, Paul W.

Conley, Martin V.
Disharoon, Jno.
Duvall, Jas. E.
Davidson, Rob't
Ewen, W. T.
Edelin, Jesse R.
Ferguson, Jno.
Field, Geo. W.
Gilroy, Thos.
Glenn, Jas. S.
Green, Wm. B.
Goodloe, Wm.
Hollingsworth, Wm. T.
Harkins, James
Hunt, Chas. W.
Hambleton, T. E.
Harwood, Rich
Jones, Rob't
Jenkins, Jas. W.
Jump, Chas. M.
Johnson, Wm.
Jarvoe, Wm. F.
Kraus, Chas. M.
Keating, Edward
Leffinger, Isaac
Lum, Benj. F.

Lancaster, Sam'l G.
Loysden, N.
Larkinson, N.
McClernney, Geo. S.
Murray, Ed. C.
Mitchell, Rob't S.
Merrick, Geo. C.
Mullin, C. S.
Moise, A. W.
Mettam, H. C.
Magruder, Ed. W.
Morris, Edwin
Morris, Lewis
Newkirk, Josiah
Paca, E. T.
Pumphrey, Jno. T.
Pumphrey, Geo. W.
Price, Wm. C.
Pollitt, Alexander
Pruitt, Jno.
Pusey, O. C.
Peeler, Mallard T.
Quinn, J. H. V.
Rich, Edward, R.
Roe, Sam'l
Ratcliffe, Edward R.

Ridgway, M. J.
Rolph, Geo. W.
Roberts, Richard
Simpson, Jno. T.
Stallings, C. L.
Schakley, H. B.
Spencer, Jno. C.
Sweeney, Geo.
Slingluff, Jno. A.
Turton, M. G.
Thompson, Charles R.
Thompson, Wm. B.
Vandiver, Geo.
Warring, Thos. G.
Welch, A. J.
Waters, Jno. A.
Worthington, H. T.
West, Joseph Jr.
Wooters, Alexander
Wood, Francis M.
Wheeler, Jas. R.
Wynn, Jas. A.
Wynn, Joseph,
Wilson, Chas.
Wright, Clinton
Ward, Archer

Co. F.

Aug. F. Schwartz, Capt.
C. Irving Ditty, 1st Lieut.
Fielder C. Slingluff, 2d Lieut.
Saml. G. Bond, 2d Lieut.
Josiah H. Slingluff, 1st Sergt.

Howard H. Kinsey, Sergt
Henry A. Wile, Sergt.
Wilbur J. Rolph, Corp.
Jno. W. Latham, Corp.
Jos. C. Shorb, Corp.

PRIVATES.

Altwater, J. W.
Ashby, R. W.
Berner, August
Bitchel, Fred F.
Beaston, Geo. M.
Breed, Hy. L.
Barnes, Jno.
Brown, Theopolus
Brown, George
Carroll, J. C.
Chaplin, Chas.
Cunningham, Geo. W.
Chapman, Isaac
Callan, Owen
Coslow, Jas.
Deaver, Jno. R.
Dooley, Thos.
Dunn, John
Eiger, Jno. H.
Flannigan, Patrick
Floyd, Wm. S.
Green, Wm.
Gardner, J. J.
Green, Hugh T.

Hummer, Joseph
Hammett, Jno. H.
Hannigan, Wm.
Hampton, Thos.
Heard, Jno. L.
Johnson, Hy. B.
Johnson, Geo.
Johnson, Jno.
Johnson, John
Kelley, Daniel B.
Kelly, Jno.
Kelly, Richard
Konig, Hy.
Kimball, Lewis
Kauffman, Carl
Leslie, Jno. W.
Lucas, H. C.
Lloyd, Jno. L.
Lusby, James
Mitchell, James
Meagher, James
Monteray, Andrew
Minnihan, Thomas
Meister, Charles

Mettee, Charles
McMullin, Charles
Ormes, Nathan
Perville, Leighton
Patton, Jas. W.
Pierce, Alfred
Pitts, William
Poole, William
Remie, Leon
Rushing, John
Rosaa, Sterling
Rose, Jesse
Sherry, Charles
Smith, Thomas
Sleighter, Benj. F.
Thacker, Albert
Tyler, Winfield
Williams, D. H. S.
Wells, William
Wilue, J. S.
Weber, Philip
Weishard, Michael
Ward, Jos.

Co. K.

Geo. R. Gaither, Capt.
Gus. W. Dorsey, Capt.
N. C. Hobbs, Capt.
Rudolph, Cecil, 1st Lieut.
George Howard, 1st Lieut.
E. H. D. Pue, 2d Lieut.
Samuel W. Dorsey, 2d Lieut.
George Howard, 2d Lieut.
Ridgely Brown, 2d Lieut.
Thomas Griffith, 2d Lieut.
Frand A. Bond, 2d Lieut.

Robert Floyd, 1st Sergt.
W. H. Wright, Sergt.
Geo. Buckingham, Sergt.
Ira Albaugh, Sergt.
W. W. Burgess, Sergt.
F. Leo Wills, Corp.
William Barnes, Corp.
B. H. Morgan, Corp.
Robert Bruce, Corp.
James Oliver, Corp.

PRIVATES.

Albaugh, Jno.
Archer, Robert
Arnett, Wm.
Bowling, C. A.
Bump, G. C.
Barry, D. R.
Bowie, H.
Bigger, Jno.
Blakely, W. H.
Brandt, A. J.
Brown, Henry
Brady, Eugene
Bowlman, M.
Barnes, William
Beatty, Edward
Betts, Samuel
Bond, F.
Bowie, W. B.
Bowie, Albert
Brown, Charles
Brown, J. W.
Brown, Lewis
Clark, Ignatius
Conradt, C. J.
Clinton, DeWitt
Clagett, H. H.
Cunningham, R.
Calbreth, Jno.
Campbell, Wm.
Carroll, Harper
Childs, Wm.
Clark, Rody,
Clements, Frank
Cook, Rudolph
Durkin, John
Davis, H. B.
Dorsey, C. R.
Dorsey, Wm.
Dusenberg, B.
Davies, Wm.
Ditty, Irving
Dorsey, C. H.
Dorsey, Hammond
Dorsey, John
Dorsey, Pue
Ellis, Thomas

Evans, Benj.
Edwards, Dr.
Fitzgerald, W. B.
Forrest, Pitt
Gill, G. M.
Griffith, Richard.
Gardner, J.
Glandel, John
Gaiging, Michael
Gaither, Washington
Gibson, Wm.
Gittings, Harry
Griffith, Frank
Griffith, Geo.
Hayden, A.
Holland, J. J. J.
Holland, P. R.
Hartmier, R.
Holland, John
Hobbs, Jarrett
Hurly, Otho
Hopkins, H.
Harding, Jno.
Hayden, Horace
Hayden, Wm.
Hewes, Wm.
Holland, Mitchell
Hobbs, Townley
Isaacs, Wm.
Jackins, Wm. K.
Jameson, Frank
Jenkins, E. D.
Jameson, James
Jenkins, Henry
Johnson, John
Kuhn, John
Keene, Robert
Kelbaugh, Wm.
Kenley, Rich
Lepper, C. V.
Logan, Alex
Linthicum, Jno.
Lambert, Wm.
Langley, Thos.
Lee, Otho S.
Le Maits, James

Merritt, Saml.
McCubbin, E.
Maguire, H. A. W.
McGinnis, Frank
Maynadier Jno. H.
Maynadier, J. M.
Mercer, E. W.
McNulty, James
McSherry, Richard
MacKall, Robert,
McCabe, Geo.
Maxwell, John
McCloud, Henry
Morton, Thos.
Murdock, Campbell
Owings, J. H.
O'Brien, E.
Offutt, John
Offutt, Wm.
Oliver, James
O'Neal, John H.
Pitts, Fred
Pitts, Jno, W.
Pitts, Wm.
Purnell, W. S.
Pitts, Emory
Plummer, John B.
Pue, Ferd
Pue, Ventress
Ridgley, Sam'l
Rinch, J. V.
Rider, Wm.
Riggs, Joshua
Roby, Townley
Smoot, Joseph
Smith, C. W.
Show, Joseph
Slater, George
Small, George
Shervill, Thos.
Smith, John
Scraggs, Robert
Smith, John
Scraggs, Robert
Sakers, John
Sisson, O. B.

Shriver, Mark O.
Schull, John
Seignor, Thos.
Sellman, John
Smith, Thomas
Stewart, Robert
Thomas, Daniel
Treackle, Albert
Tonge, Richard

Turner, Thomas
Wheatley, Chas.
Walsh, Thos.
Witzlebben, A.
Waters, Green
Waters, T. J.
Wilson, A. S.
Weeks, H.
Wilson, Chas.

Wilson, Luther
Wagner, Hy.
Wheatly, Frank
Waters, John
Webster, Wm. S.
Wheatley, Walter
Wrench, John
Wilson, Wm. S.

Some of the actions in which the First Maryland Cavalry were engaged : Kernstown, Maurytown, Greenland Gap, Oakland, Md., Morgantown, W. Va., Bridgeport, W. Va., Cairo, W. Va., Middletown, W. Va., Winchester, Va., Hagerstown, Md., Morton's Ford, Brandy Station, Auburn or Cedar Creek, Buckland, Gainesville, Taylorsville, Pollard's Farm, Old Church, Beaver Dam, Dabney's Ferry, Ashland, Trevillian's Station, Leetown, Bladensburg, Rockville, Md., Poolsville, Md., Gettysburg, Pa., Martinsburg, Va., Charlestown, Va., Bunker Hill, Va., Fisher's Hill, Va., Madison C. H., Va., Liberty Mills, Va., High Bridge, Va., Appomattox.

Cloverdale, Botetourt Co., Va., April 28th, 1865.

LIEUT.-COL. DORSEY, Commanding First Maryland Cavalry :

I have just learned from Capt. Emack, that your gallant band was moving up the Valley in response to my call. I am deeply pained to say that our army cannot be reached, as I have learned that it has capitulated. It is sad indeed to think that our country's future is all shrouded in gloom. But for you and your command there is the consolation of having faithfully done your duty. Three years ago the chivalric Brown joined my old regiment with twenty-three Maryland volunteers, with light hearts and full of fight. I soon learned to admire, respect and love them for all those qualities which endear soldiers to their officers. They recruited rapidly, and as they increased in numbers, so did their reputation and friends increase, and they were soon able to form a command and take a position of their own. Need I say when I see that position so high and almost alone among soldiers, that my heart swells with pride to think that a record so bright and glorious is in some part linked with mine, would that I could see the mothers and sisters of every member of your Battalion, that I might tell them how nobly you have represented your State, and maintained your cause.

But you will not be forgotten. The fame you have won will be guarded by Virginia with all the pride she feels in her own sons, and the ties which have linked us together, memory will preserve you who struck the first blow in Baltimore and *the last in Virginia* have done all that could be asked of you, and had the rest of our officers and men adhered to our cause with the same devotion, to-day *we would* have been free from Yankee thraldom. I have ordered the brigade to return to their homes, and it behooves us now to separate with my warmest wishes for your welfare, and a hearty God bless you, I bid you farewell.
THOMAS T. MUNFORD,
Brig.-Gen. Commanding Division.

SECOND MARYLAND CAVALRY.

No official muster rolls of this Command have been found—A partial list of officers and men in the respective Companies have been made up from memory.

FIELD AND STAFF.

Harry Gilmor, Lieut. Col.
Herman F. Keidel, Adjt.
N. W. Owings, Q. M.

Edward Williams, Sgt. Maj.
Wm. Allen, Q. M. Sgt.

Co. A.

Nicholas Burke, Capt.
W. W. McKaig, 1st Lieut.
Jno. B. Wells, 2nd Lieut.

Meredith Gilmor, 2nd Lieut.
Jos. Stansbury, 1st Sergt.
Alonzo Travers, 2nd Sergt.

PRIVATES.

Bryas, Philip
Norwood, Lewis

Dobbs,
Pendleton, Frank

Norwood, W.

Co. B.

Eugene Diggs, Capt.

Harrison, 1st Lieut.

Co. C.

David M. Ross, Capt.
Richard T. Gilmor, 1st Lieut.
Geo. Forney, 2nd Lieut.
Wm. H. Kemp, 2nd Lieut.
Frederick Baker, 1st Sergt.
M. Todd, Sergt.

Fields, Sergt.
Jno. Bosley, Sergt.
W. H. Todd, Corp.
Jno. Emmerick, Corp.
Henry Bushbaum, Corp.

PRIVATES.

Alcock, C.
Brotherton, David
Brogden, J. Sellman
Brandeberry, Jesse
Clark, Duncan
Disney, Wm.
Debrill, Chas.
Doran, Wm.
Daniels, Wm.
Devries, Wm.
Davis, Moscow
Emmart, Geo.

Ford,
Freeburger, Wm.
Gilmor, Wm. of Wm.
Glocker, Theo.
Gilmor, Hoffman
Gorsuch, N.
Hancock, N. H.
Harding,
Heimiller, Wm.
Kahler, C. P.
Murphy, Frank
Murphy, Geo.

Martin, Dr. Hugh
Miller, Henry,
Pullen, Henry
Phillips, Jno.
Powell, Geo.
Stocksdale, Geo. W.
Strausburger,
Talbot, J. F. C.
Williams, Pat.
Weaver, Henry

Co. D.

J. R. Burke, Capt.

Polk Burke, 1st Lieut.

Co. E

J. E. Sudler, Capt.

Geo. Ratcliffe, 1st Lieut.

J. C. Holmes, Sergt.

PRIVATES.

Feast, Loudon
Travers, J. M.

Hobbs, W. H.
Turpin, Thos. L.

Kelton, C. B.

Schaffer, Geo. W.
Upshur, L.

Co. F.

Jas. L. Clark, Capt.
W. H. Richardson, 1st Lieut.
Wm. Dorsey, 2nd Lieut.
E. Hurst, 2nd Lieut.
Jas. McAleese, 2nd Lieut.
J. A. Stine, 1st Sergt.
J. Sprigg, Sergt.

L. McMullin, Sergt.
R. Hahn, Sergt.
Kemp, Sergt.
T. Kidd, Sergt.
J. Andre, Corp.
C. J. Stewart, Corp.
S. C. Magraw, Corp.

PRIVATES.

Allen, Jno.
Brubake, R.
Burns, Ignatius
Bennett, Wm.
Berritt, J. T.
Bosley, J. R.
Buchanan, Thos.
Boyle, Philip
Cherry, Jas.
Castleman, C. W.
Castleman, Thos.
Chapman, Wm.
Croughan, Michael
Callen, Jno.
Cooley, Ambrose
Camble, Thos.
Carlisle, Geo.
Dunegan, Philip
Denmead, Aquilla
Dorsey, Albert
Deroies, Jno.
Favour, C. R.

Fisher, C. D.
Fipps, S.
Fitzpatrick, Dan'l
Foman, Perry
Foman, Chas.
Gillen, Stephen
Gault, C.
Gilmor, C. G.
Gilmor, Arthur
Gilmor, H.
Glenn, W. Y.
Horn, H.
Hammond, C.
Hobbs, J.
Halpin, S. P.
Hook, R. B.
Hamilton, Wm.
Harding, Jno.
Hagan, R.
Kennedy, Wm.
Loveday, Chas.
Lakins, Chas.

Logsden, Nimrood
Lamar, Rob't
Murray, Geo.
Mitchell, Jas.
Martin, Geo.
Moulton, Wm.
Moog, Jas.
Newkirk, J. V.
Pettis, A.
Peregoy, H.
Reily, F.
Reed, Wm.
Snively, G.
Scully, P.
Stine, Joseph
Thompson, Geo.
Talbert, F.
Tilghman, Jno.
Travers, J. H.
Warfield, Adolph
Winder, S.
Wood, C. S.
Zimmerman, Wm.

FIRST MARYLAND ARTILLERY.

MARYLAND.

R. SNOWDEN ANDREWS, Capt.
W. F. DEMENT, Capt.

Chas. S. Contee, 1st Lieut.
John Gale, 2d Lieut.

Frederick Y. Dabney, 2d. Lieut.
W. J. Hill, 2d Lieut.

J. H. Stonestreet, 2d Lieut.

De Wilton Snowden, 1st Sergt.
J. Harris Forbes, 1st Sergt.
F. W. Bollinger, Corp.
Theodore Jenkins, Corp.
Geo. T. Scott, Corp.

Gratial C. Thompson, 1st Sergt.
E. C. Moncure, Corp.
P. A. L. Contee, Corp.
J. G. Harris, Corp.
Jno F. Ranson, Corp.

PRIVATES.

Albert, A. J., Jr.
Aldridge, John
Boarman, Rich. T.
Bowie, Thomas D.
Brown, W. B.
Buchanan, W. J.
Boswell, Richard T.
Busk, Jerome
Brian, E. N.

Byrne, Sam. E.
Boteler, Walter P.
Bromley, Geo. W.
Briscoe, Jno H.
Bradford, T. G.
Bowie, H. C.
Basford, G. W.
Bowen, W. H.
Brooks, Thomas

Bryan, R. S.
Bowland, S. G.
Beale, Jas. S.
Blumenauer, M.
Broughton, Thos.
Barry, M. C. Y.
Buchanan, J. R.
Ballard, W. W.
Burtles, C. H.

Berry, E. R.
Bryan, Robt. S.
Coombs, G. G.
Compton, W. P.
Chiles, W. L.
Cooke, Geo. A.
Covington, Jesse H.
Coale, Wm. A.
Craven, B. L.
Campbell, John
Crowley, Jas.
Cawood, E. M.
Chew, R. B.
Conner, Wm.
Caperton, Jas. M.
Cleary, R. E.
Clayton, G. W.
Conley, Michael
Davis, John T.
Damar, John S.
Duvall, P. B.
Duvall, S. F.
Dorsey, Evan L.
Dougherty, G. A.
Diggs, J. T.
Dorsett, J. H.
Dryden, R. J.
Dorsey, Dan. H.
Dunlop, S. O.
Daffin, Francis D.
Dean, Wm. H.
Edelin, Philip F.
Edge, J. G.
Forber, Marshall A.
Ford, Jas. E.
Field, Ed. W.
Franklin, J. F.
Freayer, Fred.
Fellins, J. W.
Gardener, J. B. W.
Gardener, J. B.
Glascock, J. E.
Gale, Frank
Gale, G. G.
Glass, Rich. C.
German, M. P.
Gumby, Jno W.
Gilpin, John
Gardner, A.
Gorman, W. H.
Gough, J. H.
Garner, J. H.
Goldsboro, Chas.

Hatton, J. W. F.
Harris, C. H.
Hatton, R. H. S.
Howell, Gustavus
Howard, Washington
Hannon, L. M.
Hannon, S. B.
Handy, J. C.
Higgins, W. G.
Hunter, Fred.
Hillary, Washington
Hatton, Joseph
Harris, Joseph
Holmead, C. H.
Hilleary, G. W.
Halstead, Chas.
Harris, Jno F.
Hawkins, J. S.
Hines, J. W.
Jenkins, Louis W.
Jenkins, W. K.
Jenkins, John
Keester, W. A.
Koons, Abram
Kaester, Louis
Lee, J. C.
Lee, Richard H.
Langsdale, H. J.
Lloyd, Daniel
McClintock, Sam.
Marriott, Geo. H.
Mackenheimer, C. P.
McWilliams, J. F.
Moncure, Chas. H.
McGlone, Barney
Morgan, Thos.
Middleton, Edward
Magruder, Edward
McNeal, Chas.
McLaughlin, E. H.
Mann, Chas. S.
May, W. H.
Mockabee, Joseph
Musgrove, Thos.
Miller, H. D.
McCormick, V. M.
Mitchell, John
Mudd, E. M.
Nelson, Francis F.
Neale, Chas. N.
Nelson, C. W.
Owens, Jas. W.
Pease, Charles

Patterson, W. W.
Pollite, Nehemiah
Perrio, Geo. W.
Perrio, Albert W.
Phipp, W. E.
Pearson, Walter H.
Pennington, H.
Riddle, Chas.
Robey, Wm. S.
Rye, John M.
Richardson, Rich.
Robinson, G. W.
Sanford, Edward
Stedham, Rich.
Sleruaker, Julius.
Sindall, Harry S.
Slater, Wm. J.
Shuster, J. M.
Steno, Jos. A.
Stinchcomb, J. E.
Sloan, E. O.
Sommers, Sam.
Scharff, Jno. T.
Sunderland, Thos.
Sargeant, H. D. C.
Shirburd, W. L.
Smith, K. B.
Sutherland, G.
Scott, Thos. H.
Tucker, Jno W.
Thomas, S. S.
Thompson, Sam.
Tyler, Grafton, Jr.
Trimble, Jno D.
Thomas, J. R.
Tolson, Albert
Wade, John R.
Wooten, Wm. T.
Winters, Harry S.
Waters, Jas. F.
Wills, W. A.
Weems, Jas. N.
Worthington, Eugene
Webb, Lewis S.
Wilson, G. W.
Wilson, W. W.
Wilson, William
Wallack, R.
Wingate, T. C.
Williams, Thos.
Willson, A. M.
Yates, John R.
Young, Alexander

Battles and Actions of the First Maryland Artillery: Chickahominy Evansport, Mechanicsville, Cedar Mountain, Gaines' Mills, 2nd Manassas, Malvern Hill, Harper's Ferry, 1st Cold Harbor, 2nd Cold Harbor, Sharpsburg, Md., Hamilton's Crossing, 1st Fredericksburg, 2nd Fredericksburg, Winchester, Mine Run, Gettysburg, Pa., Turkey Ridge, Petersburg, White Sulphur Springs, Squirrel Level Road.

SECOND MARYLAND ARTILLERY.

BALTIMORE LIGHT.

JOHN B. BROCKENBOROUGH, Capt.
WILLIAM H. GRIFFIN, Capt.

Wm. B. Bean, 1st Lieut.
Jas. T. Wilhelm, 2d Lieut.

John McNulty, 1st Lieut.
J. W. Goodman, 2d Lieut.

W. Wirt Robinson, 1st Sergt.
W. Y. Glenn, Sergt.
George Poindexter, Sergt.
John F. Hayden, Sergt.
John Powers, Sergt.
Andrew J. Byrne, Sergt.

J. H. Smith, Sergt.
William C. Dunn, Corp.
Patrick Kirby, Corp.
Lewis F. Talbott, Corp.
Wm. H. Kendrick, Corp.
Jas. O'Grady, Corp.

PRIVATES.

Arens, Henry
Banner, Chas
Berger, Jos.
Bean, J. A.
Bradley, Thos. J.
Burnett, Chester C.
Bunting, John
Brockenborrough, W. M.
Burgess, John
Beane, Martin
Briscoe, R. C.
Brown, W. H.
Barry, H. C.
Bukey, C. L.
Carr, Jno. C.
Claus, Lewis
Claiborne, C. H.
Cleal, Chas.
Clotworthy, Geo. W.
Cosgriff, Jas. O.
Coffee, M. J.
Charlotte, Geo. W.
Campbell, Wm.
Chambers, John E.
Christy, G. W.
Coleman, J. A.
Cox, Geo.
Cox, W. H. H.
Dempsey, Joseph
Davis, Joshua
Davis, Wm. A.
Duvall, W. R.
Duncan, J. A.
Dosenberg, H. B.
Edle, H. J.
Evans, Chas.
Earnest, Thos. J.
Farmer, James
Fitzpatrick, John D.

Forner, Wm.
Ferry, Wm. S.
Frederick, A.
Fletcher, S. D.
Faucett, Jas. A.
Farr, F. A.
Fitzgerald, R. E.
Grady, James
Guyther, Jas. W.
Grubb, H. C.
Greenwell, J. A.
Gatchell, J. G.
Gegan, W. H.
Gordon, W. J.
Gardner, E. F.
Gibson, F.
Gibson, E.
Hammett, Daniel
Hardy, Samuel
Hammer, F. H.
Harrington, S. W. J
Hinnick, Marion
Hunter, Robert
Hurst, William
Howard, William
Hynes, Edward
Hottinger, Moses
Hart, Wm.
Hickman, Joshua
Holland, Albert
Hands, Washington
Heron, A.
Irvin, Michael
Irvin, John
Israel, G. P.
Johnson, G. M.
Johnson, Thomas
Jones William
Jackson, H. J.

Knight, John
Kuble, Adolphus
King, Jas. A.
Kernan, A.
Knight, L. W.
Knox, Wm. F.
Kelly, Wm.
Lanier, Jas. B.
Long, George E.
Lynch, Jno. P.
Lucas, Wm. J.
Long, E. J.
Legg, E. A.
Leadenborne, P.
Ladd, N. E.
Mahard, Wm.
McAviene, Chas.
McLord, Matthew
Maloney, James
Mettee, Chas. N.
Moth, E.
Mullin, C. X.
Moran, Michael G.
Monchan, Jas.
Marston, Harry
Morrison, Jas. S.
McCubbin, R. W. Jr.
McClernan, Sam
Mattison, S. J.
McAvoy, W. F.
McKinzie, E. H.
Marston, Fred
Mudd, Jno. T.
Marshall, P. B.
Mentzer, Saml.
Martin, Geo.
Malone, D.
McAlwee, Geo. W.
Naylor, W. E.

Neal, Frank
Neal, Henry
Oldson, W. H. C.
Owens, J. F.
Paine, Wm.
Pembroke, Geo.
Peake, C. Davis
Peregoy, C. E.
Pohlman, Chris
Pilert, Geo.
Quinn, Wm.
Roane, J.
Robertson, George
Reilly, John
Ross, Anthony,
Robinson, G. S.
Rheim, W. G.
Rieman, H.
Rucker, Wm.
Richardson, G. W.
Richardson, T. J.

Richardson, W.
Richardson, H.
Rogers, W. C.
Robey, H. A.
Rheim, J. J.
Rennolds, John
Raymond, C. C.
Richardson, Jr.
Smith, H. C.
Staylor, G. W.
Stout, Wm.
Shaffer, G. W.
Smith, J. E.
Shaw, J. C.
Schenberger, J. F.
Smith, W. P.
Stinson, R. J.
Shue, J. J.
Shock, W. A.
Sharkey, S.
Shaeffer, Adam F.

Stump, Geo.
Sheeker, Wm. G.
Sanner, Alex A.
Stanbaugh, J. E.
Sullivan, J. H.
Sullivan, J. D. H.
Thompson, F. M.
Tarr, William
Walter, John A.
Wilson, T. J.
Wood, W. H.
Warden, Wm.
Wales, J. C.
Whalen, W. P.
Wheeler, Albert
Watkins, N. W.
Ward, T.
Welsh, Martin
Wisong, H.
Wallace, Wm.

Some of the Battles and Actions of the Baltimore Light Artillery:
Rappahannock, Front Royal, Winchester, Bolivar Heights, Fisher's Hill, Harrisonburg, Cross Keys, Gaines' Mills, Disp tch Station, Malvern Hill, 2d Manassas, Harper's Ferry, Moorefield, Sharpsburg, Kernstown, Carlisle (Pa.), Gettysburg (Pa.), Hagerstown (Md.), Mine Run, Brandy Station, Old Town (Md.), Yellow Tavern, Martinsburg, Poolesville (Md.), Maurytown.

THIRD MARYLAND ARTILLERY.

HENRY B. LATROBE, Capt.
JOHN B. ROWAN, Capt.
WM. L. RITTER, Capt.

Ferdinand O. Claiborne, 1st Lieut.
W. Thompson Patten, Lieut.
Holmes Erwin, Lieut.

T. D. Giles, Lieut.
J. W. Duncaster, Lieut.
Thos. J. Rogers, Asst. Surg.

Rufus McCeeny, 1st Sergt.
Jas. M. J. Buchanan, Sergt.
Albert T. Emory, Sergt.
John P. Hooper, Sergt.
E. H. Langley, Sergt.
Joseph Lackey, Sergt.
L. W. Frazier, Sergt.
J. W. Smith, Sergt.
Wm. Fleming, Sergt.
Daniel Toomey, Sergt.
Benj. F. Weaver, Corp.
S. G. W. Gerding, Corp.
Jos. Edgar, Corp.
Wm. Fleming, Corp.
M: H. O'Connell, Corp.
W. H. Erwin, Corp.

G. W. Hancock, Corp.
T. H. Jones, Corp.
J. C. Pendley, Corp.
V. P. Herron, Corp.
A. J. Davis, Corp.
Wm. T. Sykes, Corp.
W. Pirkle, Corp.
B. Sanchez, Corp.
Ed. Wynn, Corp.
M. L. Welsh, Corp.
Jackson Simmons, Corp.
S. R. Sheppard, Corp.
Fredk Geiger, Bugler.
Nicholas Pirvers, Blacksmith.
Patrick McCann, Artificer.
Jos. G. Fletcher, Artificer.

W. B. P. Mills, Farrier.

PRIVATES.

Armstrong, Lewis	Dailey, W. H.	Hunter, J. P.
Aultman, N.	Duffan, Henry	Herron, B. C.
Aultman, S.	Driscoll, James	Herman, S.
Ashborne, A. R.	Downs, James	Helwig, L.
Adams, J. H.	Dwyer, Martin	Holbrook, G. J.
Byron, Timothy	Dove, W. S.	Holbrook, A.
Berg, John	Davis, W. E.	Hammond, W. H.
Burnes, Robt. B.	Donohue, Edward	Harris, G. W.
Bradford, Baldwin	Dooley, F.	Hendry, W.
Blakeslie, Chas. E.	Davidson, E.	Hattaway, W., Sr.
Bell, Wm.	Davis, W. J.	Hattaway, W., Jr.
Beverly, N. M.	Degan, Caspar	Harvey, W.
Brown, N. M.	Ellicott, Chas. J. F.	Heineman, H.
Brown, G. W.	Elder, Henry	Hunter, W.
Bushrong, J. A.	Eaton, J. H.	Isham, J. H.
Barrett, J. H.	Edwards, F. K.	Jones, S.
Bradbery, L. S.	Early, Thos.	Jones, W.
Birdwell, D. J.	Ford, Jas. W.	Johnson, G. W.
Bailey, F. M.	Fletcher, J. G.	Jackson, O.
Bridges, W.	Foley, John	Johnson, S.
Beasley, D.	Fowler, E. C.	Jones, Geo.
Blackburn, Wm.	Flener, A.	Johnson, Stephen
Butler, H. C.	Fulkerson, J. K. P.	Johnson, J. W.
Buckner, W.	Fowler, A. J.	Johnson, D. W.
Brown, A. H.	Filmer, F.	Jones, W. J. W.
Benton, John	Foley, D.	Jones, C. A.
Bennett, Wm. B.	Flowers, W. H.	Jordan, B.
Beasley, Joseph	Falk, S.	Jackson, C. G.
Burton, Mich.	Farmer, Thos	Kelly, Peter.
Bowler, Thos.	Gordon, Henry	Koburg, Chas.
Crangle, Robert	Gordrian, Antony	Kerby, Jos. A.
Connor, Alexander	Gates, W	Kelly, John
Caulk, Wm. H.	Ganst, B.	Kenn, Edward
Carrill, John	Garrett, W. A. H.	Kitzmiller, H.
Clark, Thos. B.	Gray, J. A.	Kerns, G. A.
Cook, Chas.	Gough, Jas.	Kimble, W. H.
Curran, John	Gorman, P.	Kirkland, J. T.
Carr, Patrick	Gugenheimer	King, W. K.
Cox, James	Gordrian, S.	Kelly, L.
Cosson, J. S.	Glover, W. H.	Love, Wm.
Cotter, J. J.	Gordon, H.	Light, J.
Cary, G. W.	Gates, L. R.	Lindsey, S. J.
Crider, W. R.	Griffin, B. W.	Lowry, F. M.
Cox, A. G.	Golden, H. F.	Latan, J. N.
Camp, G. W.	Golden, W.	Lynch, D.
Carberry, Patrick	Hail, Francis	Lewis, M.
Carmon, J. G.	Hogan, James	Lee, A.
Clark, T. H.	Harman, Victor	Lawless, W.
Clark, Chas.	Hinton, Nich. J.	Miller, Charles
Chafin, S.	Herman, Solomon	Mack, Thomas
Cheasham, J.	Hawley, G. W.	Miller, George
Crozart, J. A.	Hurley, C.	Morgan, Francis
Crowley, M.	Hughes, J. O.	Melton, Sam'l.
Connor, James	Hylton. S.	Mackin, James
Cousins, J. H.	Ham, James	McMahon, Jno C.
Craig, Ed.	Hoffman, J. H.	McMahon, Hugh
Cheser, G. S.	Harvey, J. C.	McKissick, J. J.
Calloway, W. A.	Hervey, W.	McCully, W.
Delaney, Francis	Holden, J.	McGuire, J.
Duvall, Chas.	Hutton, S.	Mann, S.

Melton, W.
Monteith, G. W.
McMillan, W.
Moses, J.
Melson, S.
Mitchell, Geo.
Milton, Jno
McDonald, Thos.
McCarthy, Jas.
McMahon, C.
Miller, Thadeus
Melson, W.
Myers, H.
McGovern, J.
Miller, Thos.
Monteith, M.
Markam, J.
Martin, J. G.
Markey, M.
McNab, A.
McKehan, W.
McWater, J. D.
Minter, W.
Maroney, Z. T.
Napoleon, Louis
Newton, S. M.
Newton, F. M.
Nichols, J. P.
Newton, J. W.
Owings, Joshua
O'Hanlon, J.
O'Brian, J.
O'Shields, J. P.
O'Neil, G. W.
Oliver, J. P.
O'Neil, D. P.
Owensbery, G.
Price, David
Perry, Sam. H.
Powers, Nicholas
Preston, John
Purdie, Wm. E.
Parkenson, J. S.
Peterson, N.
Pne, R. P.
Powell, J. J.
Parnill, T. A.

Price, Chas.
Perry, W.
Powell, H. B.
Parker, J. B.
Parker, Wm.
Powell, W. B.
Quinlin, Edward
Ray, M.
Reynolds, W.
Reynolds, D.
Rogers, W.
Rodrigues, Francisco
Renuolds, W.
Ryan, M.
Rogers, J. P.
Roland, D. P.
Robinson, W. A.
Robertson, J. A. G.
Robinson, Chas.
Stansbury, Jno L.
St. Clair, Albert L.
Smith, James
Simms, Willis R.
Short, James
Sullivan, John, No. 1
Stone, J. W.
Stone, A.
Stunt, R.
Singer, G.
Sullivan, Andrew
Schwan, Francis
Stewart, H. S.
Smith, J. S.
Shipley, G. R.
Sailor, M.
Savell, Thomas S.
Samms, R. J.
Scales, J. S.
Snipes, R.
Sprengling, P.
Simmons, J.
Silver, S. M.
Seawright, W. L.
Silas, D.
South, F.
Smith, Francis

Simpson, G.
Sullivan, John, No. 2
Smith, Pharis
Smith, Thomas
Stansbury, John
Shea, Timothy
Smith, J. W.
Smith, J. T.
Smith, M.
Tilyea, John
Tyson, Richard
Tyler, C.
Tinley, J.
Tomkins, E. A.
Thornton, Ed. N.
Taylor, J.
Tatton, T.
Tomlinson, T. M.
Turner, J..A.
Thomas, Geo. H.
Usery, D.
Welsh, Daniel
Willson, Thomas
Wilkins, Jno D.
Wilson, Jno S.
Wilson, James
Wells, E.
Wills, J. P.
Whalen, J.
Wills, W.
Wade, A. P.
Wilson, W.
Woodward, J.
Ware, R.
Wilson, J. J.
Weaver, John
Wills, A.
Wells, W.
Wakefield
Watkins, E.
Worall, W.
Wooten, Jos.
Whiteing, Jas.
Williams, Thomas
Young, H. L.
Zimmerman, J.

The Third Maryland Artillery was mustered into the service of the Confederate States January 14th, 1862, at Richmond, Va. Immediately sent to Knoxville, Tenn. Served under Gen. E. Kirby Smith in the Campaigns in Tennessee and Kentucky, being the advance battery from Lexington, Ky., to within three and a half miles of Covington. After the retreat from Kentucky, was sent to Vicksburg under Gen. Stevenson, one section commanded by Lieut. W. T. Patten manned the guns of the Ram Queen of the West, when the Indianola was captured. All except four were lost, when the Queen was burned, one detachment under Lieut. Wm. L. Ritter, served under Col. G. W. Ferguson on Deer Creek, during which time it assisted in capturing a large Federal transport. It afterwards served under Gen. Johnston in the battle before Jackson,

Miss. Three detachments remained at Vicksburg and participated in the battle of Baker's Creek and were besieged at Vicksburg and there taken prisoners. Seventy-seven were paroled and furloughed, after being exchanged. Reorganized in September 1862. The Company again ready for active service. Went to the front at Sweetwater, Tenn., October 2d, 1863. Thence to Lookout Mountain, thence to Missionary Ridge and commenced the retreat to Dalton, Ga. On the night of the 24th this command from its organization to the present time, has never lost a gun except, at the surrender at Vicksburg. The Company's last muster was at Meridan, Miss., May 10th, 1865.

FOURTH MARYLAND ARTILLERY.

CHESAPEAKE.

WILLIAM BROWN, Capt.
WALTER S. CHEW, Capt.

Jno. E. Plater, 1st Lieut.

Jas. D. Wall, 1st Sergt.
Rob't A. Crowley, Sergt.
Philip H. H. Brown, Sergt.
Jno. P. Hickey, Sergt.
Jos. H. Ennis, Sergt.
Henry C. Buckmaster, Sergt.
Thos. W. Mummey, Corp.
Geo. A Smith, Corp.

Benj. G. Roberts, 2nd Lieut.

Henry Baker, Corp.
Isaac J. Blunt, Corp.
Geo. C. Phillips, Corp.
Thos. G. Jackson, Corp.
F. M. Fairbanks, Corp.
Dan'l A. Wilkinson, Bugler.
Michael H. Brady, Artificer.
A. J. Covington, Artificer.

PRIVATES.

Acton, Washington
Brady, Michael H.
Brown, Jno. W.
Barchuss, W. W.
Burke, W. L.
Canfield, Jno. H.
Covington, Allen J.
Cottrell, Edward C.
Cook, Jacob F.
Carberry, Thos. A.
Culver, E. K.
Corry, H.
Dawson, Lambdin T.
Dallam, Chas. F.
Denn, Jas. E.
Dean, Thos.
Evergan, Thos. J.
Egan, Andrew H.
Ennis, Thos. H.
Fairbank, Francis M.
Gardener, Jno. H.
Green, Vincent
Green, Jno. F.
Gore, Jno. W.
Goodhand, G. W.
Green, A.
Grimes, Rob't
Hill, Jno.

Harrison, Philip L.
Harper, Jas. K.
Hoof, Jno. J.
Huber, Paul
Holtzman, Wm. H. F.
Hermantrout, W. F.
Jackson, Thos. G.
Kirby, Francis M.
Loud, Jno. J.
Lynch, Christopher G.
Langley, Richard E.
Lane, Jno. A.
Mowbry, Jno. K.
Mason, Wm. H.
McCubbin, Geo. B.
McCure, Thos.
Myers, Jno.
McClure, Geo. D.
McElwee, Andrew J.
Moore, Jas. T.
Mettee, C.
Maccummins, F.
Oldson, Wm.
Pratt, Jas. P.
Pinder, Wm.
Porter, Grstavus
Peters, Jno. L.
Phillips, Sam'l W.

Parker, Peter H.
Perry, Jno. G.
Renshaw, Wm. T.
Richardson, Nicholas T.
Richardson, Jno. D.
Raley, Michael N.
Rice, Geo.
Russell, Henry
Randill, J.
Sparks, Jas. S.
Stewart, Jas. P.
Spencer, Bendinfield
Smith, Wm.
Shannahan, Jno. H. H.
Suit, Norris N.
Stewart, Francis M.
Trigger, Wm.
Tarbutton, Wm.
Toy, Thos. B.
Tinges, Chas. J.
Triggoe, C. P.
Williams, Wm. M.
Webb, Richard W.
Warrington, Smith
Wilson, Jas. H.
Young, Benj.
Yates, W. F.

Some of the engagements of the Fourth Maryland Artillery, Chesapeake: Fredericksburg, Seven Pines, Gettysburg, 2nd Manassas, Hanover Junction, Cedar Mountain, Seven Days Around Richmond, Frederick's Hall, Sharpsburg, Harper's Ferry, Winchester, Yellow Tavern, Petersburg.

ROSTER

OF

OFFICERS AND MEMBERS,

OF THE

SOCIETY OF THE

Army and Navy of the Confederate States.

In the State of Maryland,

Incorporated and Recorded in Liber G. R., No. 19, Folio 294, one of the Charter Records of Baltimore City,

WITH

CONSTITUTION.

BALTIMORE,

JANUARY, 1894.

OFFICERS OF THE SOCIETY.

1894.

President:

BRIG. GENL. BRADLEY T. JOHNSON.

Vice-Presidents:

CAPT. GEO. W. BOOTH,
CAPT. GEO. R. GAITHER,
MAJOR MASON MORFIT,
MAJOR H. ASHTON RAMSEY,
ENGINEER EUGENE H. BROWNE,
LIEUT. CHAS. H. CLAIBORNE,

PRIVATE HUGH McWILLIAMS,
LIEUT. H. M. GRAVES,
LIEUT. COL. J. LYLE CLARKE,
SERGT. CHAS. KETTLEWELL,
PRIVATE D. RIDGELEY HOWARD,
PRIVATE M. B. BROWN.

Recording Secretary:

CAPT. AUGUSTINE J. SMITH.

Asst. Recording Secretary:

PRIVATE JOSHUA THOMAS.

Corresponding Secretary:

PRIVATE JOHN F. HAYDEN.

Treasurer:

CAPT. F. M. COLSTON.

Executive Committee:

PRIVATE JAMES R. WHEELER,
SERGT. WM. H. POPE,
PRIVATE AUGUST SIMON,

MASTERS MATE W. H. FITZGERALD.
MAJOR W. STEUART SYMINGTON,
PRIVATE D. L. THOMAS,

PRIVATE MARK O. SHRIVER.

Chaplains:

REV. W. U. MURKLAND, SERGT. MAJOR.
" B. F. BALL, SERGT.
" R. W. COWARDIN, (S. J.) SERGT.
" WM. M. DAME, PRIVATE.

Sergeant at Arms:

SERGT. GEO. W. SCHAFER.

CONSTITUTION

OF THE

Society of the Army and Navy

OF THE

CONFEDERATE STATES,

IN THE STATE OF MARYLAND.

———•◦•———

CHAPTER I.

To collect and preserve the material for a truthful history of the late War between the Confederate States and the United States of America ; to honor the memory of our Comrades who have fallen ; to cherish the ties of friendship among those who survive, and to fulfil the duties of sacred charity towards those who may stand in need of them—we whose names are appended do hereby associate ourselves together for the purpose named, and do adopt for our government the following Constitution :

SECTION 1. The name of our Society shall be " The Society of the Army and Navy of the Confederate States, in the State of Maryland."

SEC. 2. All persons shall be eligible to membership who honorably served in the Army or Navy of the Confederate States until the close of the war, or were honorably discharged therefrom.

SEC. 3. All male descendants of those who honorably served in the Army and Navy of the Confederate States until the close of the war, or were honorably discharged therefrom, upon arriving at the age of fifteen years, upon satisfactory proof, shall be entitled to membership, but without a vote until arriving at the age of eighteen years.

SEC. 4. Members of kindred societies in other States may be elected honorary members by a vote of this Society.

SEC. 5. The election of honorary members shall be *viva voce* upon the nomination of the General Committee, and shall confer no privilege beyond that of attending meetings and reunions of the Society, without a vote.

SEC. 6. Active members who have ceased to contribute to the support of the Society, while in arrears, shall be considered and denominated Passive members, and be debarred the privilege of participating in the meetings of the Society.

SEC. 7. Applications for membership shall be addressed to the Corresponding Secretary, and shall be made in accordance with a printed form to be prescribed for the purpose by the General Committee, and shall set forth briefly the military or naval record of the applicant, accompanied by satisfactory proofs of honorable service.

SEC. 8. The record furnished by each member elected at the time of his application shall be copied into a book to be kept for the purpose ; and in order that said records may be uniform and complete, original members of the Society shall furnish to the Recording Secretary similar statements, prepared according to the same form.

SEC. 9. Applications when received shall be referred to the General Committee, by whom they shall be considered and voted upon, each applicant being balloted for separately, and one-third of those present being sufficient to defeat any application.

SEC. 10. All persons who are in entire sympathy with our cause are eligible to auxiliary membership upon the payment of five dollars initiation fee and two dollars per annum, without a vote.

SEC. 11. The officers of the Society shall be a President, twelve Vice-Presidents, one Recording Secretary, one Assistant, one Corresponding Secretary, a Treasurer, four Chaplains, and an Executive Committee of seven, all of whom shall be elected annually, and who shall constitute together the General Committee.

SEC. 12. The Executive Committee shall make arrangements for the general meetings and annual reunions, also for the proper observance of Memorial Days, and for the expenditure of the funds of the Society for the payment of current expenses and charitable purposes, and all other business of the Society. The committee shall meet on the call of the President, who with the Secretary shall be ex-officio members. Three members shall constitute a quorum.

SEC. 13. The General Committee, of which the President shall be ex-officio chairman, shall meet on the call of the President for the purpose of disposing of applications for membership. Seven members a quorum.

SEC. 14. The annual meeting shall be held on the 3rd Tuesday in December, at such time and place as the Executive Committee shall designate.

SEC. 15. General meetings may be held at other times on the call of the Executive Committee.

SEC. 16. The amount of dues shall be one dollar per annum, in advance.

SEC. 17. The Executive Committee shall adopt all necessary by-laws not inconsistent with the provisions of this Constitution and the general objects of this Society.

SEC. 18. This Constitution shall not be altered in whole or in part except by a vote of two-thirds of those present, and voting at a general meeting; thirty day's previous notice required.

SEC. 19. Societies of Confederate Soldiers or Sailors in Maryland may become members of this Society and entitled to representation therein.

SEC. 20. The Vice-Presidents in the absence of the President shall preside in the order of the vote by which they were elected. The Recording Secretary shall have charge of all records and documents. The Executive Committee, the General Committee and Treasurer shall make reports at the annual meeting.

SEC. 21. The Badge of the Society shall be as heretofore adopted—the Battle-Flag of the Confederate States, three-quarters of an inch square, in red and blue enamel, the field red, the cross blue, and the stars and border of cross and flag of silver. In the upper quarter, 1861; in the lower quarter, 1865. This square attached to the three upper arms of the Maryland Cross, which shall be of blue enamel, bordered with silver, and on it the letters A. and N. C. S., Md.; the whole suspended by a heavy silk ribbon, three-quarters of an inch wide, divided perpendicularly into equal red and white stripes, one-half being red and the other half white, the whole fastened with a silver clasp or buckle, one inch wide one way and one-quarter wide the other.

The seal shall consist as now used, of the Saltier Cross, from the battle-flag, thirteen stars. In the top quarter the figures 1861; in the bottom quarter the figures 1865; in the left-hand quarter the word "Deo;" in the right hand quarter the word "Vindice;" the whole surrounded with a circle, in which shall be the official name of the Society, and the date, 1871.

Society of the Army and Navy

——OF THE——

Confederate States, in the State of Maryland.

———

The Society of the Army and Navy of the Confederate States in the State of Maryland, was organized in 1871, "To collect and preserve the material for a truthful history of the late war between the Confederate States and the United States of America; to honor the memory of our comrades who have fallen; to cherish the ties of friendship among those who survive, and to fulfil the duties of sacred charity toward those who may stand in need of them."

In 1874, with the aid of an appropriation from the State of Maryland, the bodies of the Marylanders who fell in the Confederate service, were gathered from all the battle-fields from Petersburg to Gettysburg. Comrades were employed for this purpose, and brave soldiers were taken from fence corners and hedge rows where they had been laid years ago. These bodies were reinterred in the Confederate lot in Loudon Park Cemetery, where are erected the central monument, "The Confederate Soldier," by Volck, and the monuments to Companies H and A of the First and Second Maryland Infantry, and that dashing Cavalryman, Lieut.-Col. Harry Gilmor. This beautiful burial plot contains about 400 bodies. It is the property of the Society, and provision has been made for its perpetual care by payments to the Cemetery Company. About $10,000 has been expended upon this work. The bodies of all the Confederate prisoners who died in Baltimore are also buried in our lot, and each grave is marked with a marble headstone, with the name, regiment and State, whenever known, of the soldier who sleeps beneath. Since 1873, the Society has always arranged for the observance of Memorial Day, June 6th, when hundreds of ladies and our comrades are conveyed to Loudon Park Cemetery to strew flowers on the graves of our dead, and the graves of our soldiers and sailors in other cemeteries also receive like attention.

In 1878 about $1,000 was realized, by means of a Music Festival, for the Lee Monument at Richmond.

In 1880 a life-size statue of a Maryland Confederate Infantry Soldier was erected by the Society in the Maryland lot in the Stonewall Cemetery at Winchester, Va.

In 1882 a donation of above $600 was made to the Southern Historical Society, Richmond, Va., which enabled that Society to continue its work at that time.

In 1885 a Bazar, held under the auspices and patronage of the Society, realized about $31,000, which was invested in an annuity fund, terminating in twenty-five years, producing a present annual income of about $2,200, which is distributed in cash to needy and worthy comrades, and is also used for the burial of the dead. No Confederate soldier is denied assistance while living, nor permitted, in death, to lie in a pauper's grave. No matter how unfortunate his circumstances in life, a respectful burial, with proper attendance, in the Confederate lot is accorded him. The Beneficial Association of the Maryland Line also dispenses among its needy members, or their families, about $1,000 per annum, making total disbursements each year nearly $4,000.

In 1886 a monument was erected on Culp's Hill, Gettysburg, to the Second Maryland Infantry. It is a massive granite block, costly and imposing, and its inscriptions testify the valor of the men who fought where it stands.

In 1888 the former United States Arsenal Buildings at Pikesville were secured from the Legislature of Maryland as a Confederate Home, with an appropriation of $5,000 a year. The rooms have been furnished as memorial offerings, and the Home now shelters inmates from different States, but citizens of Maryland at time of entry.

From time to time many addresses have been delivered by distinguished Confederates, and numerous pamphlets have been published by the Society.

The only stated public appearances of the Society are at the Annual Banquets and on Memorial Days. It has made no public parades, except on the occasions of dedications of monuments at Richmond, Lexington, Winchester, Front Royal, Staunton, Hagerstown, Frederick and Gettysburg, or at the funerals of distinguished comrades.

The Society now numbers above 1,050 members, the annual dues being $1.00. An accurate record of each member, certified by commanding officers or comrades, is entered in the Historical Register of the Society, and it is intended that this Register and Roster shall be finally deposited with the Maryland Historical Society. No unworthy soldier or deserter is permitted to become a member.

The sons of Confederate Soldiers and Sailors are entitled to membership in the Society as "Male Descendants," upon arriving at the age of fifteen years.

All persons who are in sympathy with our cause, but who were not in the service of the Confederate States, are eligible to "Auxiliary Membership."

The successive Presidents have been:

Major-General ISAAC R. TRIMBLE,	-	-	1871.
Major JOHN R. McNULTY,	-	- -	1875.
Lieutenant McHENRY HOWARD,	-	-	1877.
Brig.-General BRADLEY T. JOHNSON,	-	-	1883.

NAME.	RANK.	BRANCH OF SERVICE.	ADDRESS.
Ackler, Wm. F.	Private	Co. D, 1st Maryland Infantry	116 Aisquith St.
Adams, James A.	Private	Co. I, 44th N. C. Infantry	Washington, Beaufort Co., N. C.
Adic. Hugh.	Lieutenant	Co. A, 9th Virginia Cavalry	
Ahern, Frank, I.	Private	Cobb's Legion	Laurel, Md.
Allison, Richard T.	Major	C. S. Marine Corps	
Allison, W. W. (M. D.)	Private	Co. F, 10th Virginia Infantry	Hagerstown, Md.
Allston, Joseph B.	Captain	Co. F, 27th S. C. Infantry	
Alvey, John F.	Major	Echol's Brigade	
Albert, A. J.	Private	1st Maryland Artillery	13 W. Chase St.
Allen, Thomas M.	Lieutenant	Co. E, 4th N. C. Infantry	Aurora, Beaufort Co., N. C.
Aldridge, Geo. W.	Sergeant	Co. C, 1st S. C. Infantry	Baltimore, Md.
Alexander, Geo. W.	Colonel	C. S. A.	Montpelier, P. G. Co., Md.
Anderson, John H.	Private	1st Richmond Howitzers.	
Anderson, R. T.	Private	2nd Maryland Infantry	Davidsonville, A. A. Co. Md.
Annan, Roberdeau.	Private	2nd Virginia Infantry	137, Linden Ave.
Anthon, Wm. E.	Private	Co. A, Fredericksburg Artillery	527 Oliver Place.
Andrews, R. Snowden.	Lieutenant-Colonel	Andrew's Artillery	107 W. North Ave.
Arnold. Charles A.	Sergeant	Co. A, 1st Maryland Infantry	1636 E. Fayette St.
Arnold, Samuel B.	Private	Co. A, 1st Maryland Infantry	2414 Hudson.
Ashley, C. B.	Private	Co. K, 34th Virginia Infantry	213 S. Vincent.
Atkinson, Archibald (M. D.)	Surgeon and Major	Pegram's Brigade	2101 Maryland Ave.
Atzeoradt, Henry	Private	Co. I, 2nd Maryland Infantry	1126 Patterson Ave.
Aubrey, James L	Private	Co. E, 2nd Maryland Infantry	504 E. Baltimore St.
Atkinson, W. G.	Lieutenant	Engineers A. N. V.	M. L. C. S. H.
Bailey, Sydnor	Sergeant	40th Virginia Infantry	639 Dolphin St.
Baker, Henry W.	Private	1st Maryland Cavalry	1730 Federal St.
Baldwin, Joseph S. (M. D.)	Private	McClanahan's Battery	Elko, Baltimore Co., Md.
Baldwin, W. B.	Private	Co. I, 26th Virginia Infantry	Brooklyn, A. A. Co., Md.
Ball, Rev. Benj. F.	Sergeant	43d Virginia Cavalry	Leesburg, Va.
Barnes, J. T. M.	Major	Trans-Mississippi-Department	1517 Park Ave.
Barnes, Jacob S.	Private	7th Virginia Cavalry	2125 E. Baltimore St.
Barnette, D. P.	Lieutenant	Co. A, 26th Virginia Infantry	Catonsville, Balto. Co. Md.
Barry, Philip.	Private	Co. A, 2nd Maryland Infantry	3 E. Read St.
Bartholomew, T. J.	Corporal	Co. E, 7th Tennessee Infantry	504 N. Gay St.

NAME	RANK	BRANCH OF SERVICE	ADDRESS
Barton, Bolling W.	Lieutenant	1st Foreign Battalion	Pikesville, Balto. Co., Md.
Barton, Randolph	A. A. General	Stonewall Brigade	207 N. Calvert St.
Baxter, George O	Private	Cooper's Battery	Bay View.
Baxter, T. W	Lieutenant	15th Texas Infantry	
Baylor, R. B	Private	Co. G, 6th Virginia Infantry	904 Park Ave.
Bayne, Wm. H	Sergeant	Brook's Artillery	
Barnes, Geo. D	Color Bearer	Co. K, 9th Virginia Infantry	402 W. 25th St.
Barney, Joseph N	Lieutenant Commander	Confederate States Navy	
Bailey, James T	Private	Co. B, 2nd Maryland Infantry	Rock Point, Charles Co., Md.
Barrett, Geo. W	Private	Co. H, 3rd Virginia Infantry	M. L. C. S. H.
Bailey, Wm. L	Major	Gen'l Joseph E. Johnston's Staff	M. L. C. S. H.
Bales, J. K	Private	Co. E, 2nd Kentucky Cavalry	815 Light St.
Beall, Henry D	Private	Co. B, 12th Virginia Cavalry	600 N. Charles St.
Bell, Alexander T. M. D	Surgeon	Stuart's Horse Artillery	9 E. Read St.
Bell, Douglas	Private	Co. G, 6th Virginia Infantry	210 N. Gilmor St.
Bennett, Edward W., Jr	Private	Co. F, 1st Maryland Infantry	128 N. Bond St.
Bennett, John W	Lieutenant	Confederate States Navy	Sykesville, Carroll Co., Md.
Bennett, L. O	Private	Stuart's Artillery	1355 York Road
Bennett, Thos. J	Private	Co. G, 34th N. C. Infantry	904 Madison Ave.
Berry, Alexander C	Lieutenant	Co. H, 1st Virginia Infantry	2106 Vine St.
Berry, Geo. W	Lieutenant	Co. H, 15th Virginia Infantry	229 S. Fremont Ave.
Berry, W. H	Sergeant	Co. B, 30th Virginia Infantry	
Berryman, John B	Sergeant	Co. C, 1st Maryland Infantry	1021 N. Stricker St.
Besant W. T	Private	Co. B, 35th Virginia Cavalry	Frederick City, Md.
Best, H. S	Sergeant	2d Georgia Infantry	1605 W. Lexington St.
Bean, H. H	Lieutenant	Co. I, 1st Maryland Infantry	M. L. C. S. H.
Beaston, Geo. M	Private	Co. F, 1st Maryland Cavalry	Locust Grove, Kent Co., Md.
Bean, W. B	Lieutenant-Colonel	Baltimore Light Artillery	Daggers Springs, Va.
Beasley, Wm. F	Private	71st North Carolina Infantry	1105 W. Lanvale St.
Bestor, Rollin J	Private	Co. I, 19th Virginia Cavalry	Bridgeport, Conn.
Belton, Patrick	Private	Co. C, 38th Virginia Artillery	M. L. C. S. H.
Billopp, Christopher	Private	Co. C, 1st Maryland Cavalry	
Biays, George	Private	Co. C, 1st Maryland Cavalry	318 Courtland St.
Bispham, Stacy B	Sergeant	Co. E, 43rd Virginia Cavalry	1303 John St.

NAME.	RANK.	BRANCH OF SERVICE.	ADDRESS.
Birch, James H	Private	Co. K, 2nd Kentucky Infantry	Macon, Ga.
Blake, Francis	Private	Co. E, 1st Maryland Infantry	1131 Valley St.
Block, Meyer J	Private	Missouri Border Guards	221 S. Eden St.
Blumenauer, John N	Private	Co. C, 2nd Maryland Infantry	1429 E. Eager St.
Blundon, Robert M	Corporal	Virginia Mil. Inst. Cadets	1047 W. Lanvale St.
Bond, Benj. F	Private	Co. A, 2nd Maryland Infantry	B. & O. Central Bldg., Balto.
Bond, Frank A	A. A. General	General Liventhrope's Staff	Jessups Cut, A. A. Co.
Bond, Frank E	Sergeant	17th Texas Infantry	1505 Presstman St.
Boone, Daniel A	Private	Ashby's Cavalry	919 N. Calvert St.
Booth, Geo. W	A. A. General	Maryland Line	B. & O. Central Bldg., Balto.
Boarman, R. T.	Private	1st Maryland Artillery	Bryantown, Charles Co., Md.
Booker, Wm. D., M. D.	Private	Co. K, 3rd Virginia Cavalry	851 Park Ave.
Bond, Arthur W	Sergeant Major	1st Maryland Cavalry	Dayton, Ohio.
Bratton, James G	Musician	1st Virginia Infantry	611 W. Baltimore St.
Breedlove, J. W	Private	Co. I, 55th Infantry	123 W. Saratoga St.
Brehm, John P	Private	Co. C, 1st Maryland Cavalry	510 Callender Alley.
Brent, Geo. T	Private	Co. B, 1st Maryland Cavalry	Piscattawa, PrinceGeorgeCo., Md
Brent, Hugh	Private	Co. A, 7th Virginia Cavalry	1805 Bolton St.
Brent, Wm. H	Private	Co. D, 9th Virginia Cavalry	
Brien, Luke Tiernan	Colonel	Staff General W. H. F. Lee	Urbana, Frederick Co., Md.
Briscoe, John H	Private	1st Maryland Artillery	421 St. Paul St.
Brogden, Sellman	Private	2nd Maryland Cavalry	Davidsonville. A. A. Co., Md.
Brooke, Geo W	Sergeant	Co. E, 1st Maryland Cavalry	Leeland, Prince George Co., Md.
Brown, John Wilcox	Major	Ordnance Department Virginia	208 E. German St.
Brown, M. B	Private	Co. H, 4th Virginia Cavalry	1416 Harlem Ave.
Browne, W. Judson	Lieutenant	Poagues Artillery	1517 Bolton St.
Browne, Eugene H	Assistant Engineer	Confederate States Navy	520 N. Gilmor St.
Bryan, T. A.	Captain	Bryans Battery	
Bryce, John C.	Corporal	Co. D, South Carolina Cavalry	Greenville. S. C.
Brooke, Robert M	Private	McGregor's Battery	416 N. Carrollton Ave.
Brooks, Richard L	Sergeant	47th Virginia Infantry	120 W. 21st St.
Briscoe, John L	Captain and A. Quartermaster	Mahone's Division	M. L. C. S. H.
Brashaers, Thos. B	Lieutenant	Tallassec Guards	Milton, Fla.
Brent, Joseph I			

NAME.	RANK.	BRANCH OF SERVICE.	ADDRESS.
Briscoe, Richard C.	Private	Baltimore Light Artillery	M. L. C. S. H.
Brooks, J. R.	Lieutenant	Co. C, 26th Virginia Infantry	318 Hanover St.
Brown, Richard L.	Sergeant	Co. C, 2nd Maryland Cavalry	15 E. Camden St.
Brattan, James H.	Sergeant	Co A, 1st N. C. Infantry	1031 William St.
Browne, R. Bernard	Private	Co. G, 7th Virginia Cavalry	1218 Madison Avenue.
Buck, Irving A.	A. A. General	Cleburnes Division	2 W. 20th St.
Buckley, John	Private	Co. F, 19th Virginia Infantry	1110 Homewood Avenue.
Burgwyn, Wm. H. S.	A. A. General	Clingman's Brigade	Henderson, N. C.
Burke, John	Private	Co. A, 2nd Maryland Cavalry	Waverly, Baltimore.
Burnham, James H.	Private	Co. B, White's Cavalry	612 Second St.
Burton, R. C.	Private	Otey Battery	1135 Harlem Avenue.
Butler, James R.	Private	Co. D, 15th Virginia Cavalry	529 N. Calhoun St.
Bussey, James T.	Captain	Co. H, 2nd Maryland Infantry	
Buck, Samuel D.	Captain	Co. H, 13th Virginia Infantry	209 E. Mt. Royal Avenue.
Bunting, John H.	Private	Co. I, 1st S. C. Infantry	
Burgess, J. W.	Private	Baltimore Light Artillery	Hancock, Md.
Burwell, Philip L.	Captain	Regular Infantry C. S. A.	Mt. Savage, Allegheny Co., Md.
Byers, Wm.	Private	Co. G, 1st Maryland Infantry	Staunton, Va.
Carey, Alexander G.	Sergeant	43rd Virginia Cavalry	2127 Maryland Avenue.
Cary, T. W.	Sergeant	2nd Maryland Cavalry	205 W. West St.
Carr, Thomas	Sergeant	1st Maryland Infantry	514 Ensor St.
Carrington, Eugene	Quartermaster	Richmond, Va.	210 E. Lexington St.
Carroll, Harper	Lieutenant	Staff of General Ewell	Doughoreghan, Howard Co.,Md.
Carroll, Wm. S.	Private	Norfolk Light Artillery, Blues.	Phoenix, Baltimore Co. Md.
Carter, H. M.	Sergeant	44th Virginia Infantry	1043 Guilford Avenue.
Cary, John B.	Private	Co. A. 1st Maryland Cavalry	4 S. Gay St.
Cary, Wilson M	Captain	Staff Genl. Joseph E. Johnston	915 N. Charles St.
Cauthorn, R. A.	Private	Co. F, 9th Virginia Cavalry	1530 N. Mount St.
Castle, James L.	Private	Co. C, 2nd Maryland Infantry	1207 Myrtle Avenue.
Campbell, Wm. H. H., M. D.	Hospital Steward	Co. F, 10th Virginia Infantry	Owings Mills.
Carter, Wm. Fitzhugh	Lieutenant	Confederate States Navy	City Hall.
Carrol, G. T.	Private	Co. F, 9th Virginia Cavalry	1019 N. Stricker St.
Chambers, John E.	Sergeant	Baltimore Light Artillery	M. L. C. S. H.
Chambers, Robert M	Private	Co. C, 1st Maryland Cavalry	1514 John St.

NAME.	RANK.	BRANCH OF SERVICE.	ADDRESS.
Chapman, John W.	Private	2nd Virginia Infantry	1703 Lemon St.
Chapman, N., M. D.	Lieutenant	Co. E, 1st Maryland Calvary	Perrymansville, Md.
Chisolm, Julian J., M. D.	Surgeon	Confederate States Army	114 W. Franklin St.
Chowning, Wm. B.	Private	Johnson's Artillery	804 Hopkins Place.
Christian, J. H., M. D.	Private	Co. D, Mosby's Cavalry	1801 Madison Ave.
Christian, John D.	Private	Pamunkey Artillery	921 Edmondson Ave.
Chalmers, J. W.	Private	Co. A, 8th Virginia Infantry	1119 W. Mulberry St.
Christian, Wm. S.	Private	3rd Virginia Cavalry	816 Cathedral St.
Chew, R. B.	Sergeant	1st Maryland Artillery	
Chalard, Frederick	Commander	Confederate States Navy	St. Louis, Mo.
Chew, R. Preston	Lieutenant Colonel	Stewart's Artillery	Charlestown, W. Va.
Clagett, Geo. H.	Private	Co. F, 2nd Maryland Infantry	Pomonkey, Charles Co. Md.
Clagett, J. T. W.	Private	Co. F, 2nd Maryland Infantry	Pomonkey, Charles Co. Md.
Claiborne, Chas. H	Lieutenant	1st South Carolina Infantry	1111 Franklin St.
Clark, Duncan C	Private	2nd Maryland Cavalry	803 Park Ave.
Clark, Frank P.	Captain	Staff Duty	111 W. 20th St.
Clark, Matthew	Lieutenant	Co. G, 13th Virginia Infantry	
Clark, Michael R.	Private	Purcell Battery	
Clarke, J. Lyle	Lieutenant Colonel	30th Virginia Infantry	2205 Oak St.
Clarke, Powhatan	Lieutenant Colonel	General Buckner's Command	605 N. Charles St.
Clay, James W.	Private	Co. G, 18th Virginia Infantry	648 W. Saratoga St.
Clendinen, Thos. R	Private	Cadets V. M. I	27 E. Mt. Vernon Place.
Closc, James	Private	Co. B, 21st Virginia Infantry	Brunswick, Baltimore, Md.
Clowe, J. N.	Sergeant	Co. C, 2nd N. C. Infantry	862 W. Fayette St.
Clinton, H. DeWitt	Private	Co. K, 1st Virginia Cavalry	M. L. C. S. H.
Clabaugh, Fenton B.	Private	Co. C, 1st Maryland Infantry	106 E. Saratoga St.
Clark, James	Private	Co. A, 1st Maryland Cavalry	118 N. Calhoun St.
Coleman, John	Private	2nd Maryland Artillery	
Collins, J. W	Private	1st Maryland Infantry	117 Harrison St.
Colston, Fred M	Captain	Ass't to Chief Ord officer A. N. V.	1016 St. Paul St.
Conradt, C. J.	Private	1st Maryland Infantry	1215 W. Lanvale St.
Conoway, W. H.	Private	Co. B, White's Cavalry	M. L. C. S. H.
Cook, Frederick	Private	Co. I, 8th Kentucky Cavalry	15 W. Hill St.
Cook, Jacob F.	Private	4th Maryland Artillery	1611 W. Fayette St.

Name.	Rank.	Branch of Service.	Address.
Cooke, Adolphus	Lieutenant	Co. B, 1st Maryland Infantry	30 S. Holliday St.
Cooper, James	Sergeant	Co. C, 1st Regiment Eng.	13 E. Lanvale St.
Copeland, Phillip D.	Private	Co. B, 12th Virginia Cavalry	29 Loudon Ave.
Cottingham, James T.	Lieutenant	5th Georgia Reserves	
Conrad, J. M. M.	Private	Co. B, 12th Virginia Cavalry	857 N. Fulton Ave.
Compton, Wm. P.	Sergeant	1st Maryland Artillery	M. L. C. S. H.
Collins, John	Private	Co. B, Marine Corps	M. L. C. S. H.
Conrad, Peter M.	Private	Co. F, 10th Virginia Infantry	Reisterstown, Balto Co., Md.
Cottrell, Edward C.	Private	4th Maryland Artillery	Dranesville, Va.
Cowardin, W. R., Rev. S. J.	Sergeant	3rd Virginia Regulars	Loyola College, Baltimore, Md.
Connolly, Patrick	Sergeant	1st South Carolina Infantry	
Cooksey, Wm. T.	Private	Co. C, 2nd Maryland Infantry	1112 Clifton Place.
Conley, Wm.	Private	Co. G, White's Cavalry	M. L. C. S. H.
Cralle, Richard K.	Private	Signal Service	Keyser Building, Baltimore.
Crane, Chas. T.	Sergeant	2nd Richmond Howitzers	407 N. Charles St.
Crane, Henry R.	Private	2nd Richmond Howitzers	242 W. Hoffman St.
Cranford, Geo. l.	Private	Co. E, 1st Maryland Cavalry	Baltimore.
Craver, Moses M.	Private	King William Artillery	218 S. Charles St.
Cridlin, Jacob H.	Lieutenant	Co. A, 30th Virginia Infantry	1553 Aisquith St.
Cridlin, Thos. L.	Sergeant	Co. F, 30th Virginia Infantry	1910 Druid Hill Ave.
Croue, Michael	Private	Co. C, 1st Virginia Regulars	311 Preston St.
Crouch, F. Nicholls, Prof.	Private	1st Richmond Howitzers	Cor. Penn and King Sts.
Cryer, J. F.	Private	Co. F, 40th Virginia Infantry	M. L. C. S. H.
Crabtree, Albert P.	Private	Co. C, Freeman's N. C. Batal.	333 St. Paul St.
Crofton, James L.	Private	Co. B, 24th Virginia Cavalry	Salada, Middlesex Co., Va.
Cross, C. Louis	Sergeant	Co. A, Davis Cavalry	225 Gorsuch Ave.
Cunningham, R. H.	Private	Co. K, 1st Virginia Cavalry	1832 Division St.
Dall, H. McPherson	Private	Co. B, 21st Virginia Infantry	2 E. Franklin St
Dandridge, P. P.	Lieutenant	9th Virginia Cavalry	
Davies, Wm. T.	Lieutenant	Co. C, 47th Virginia Infantry	308 W. Lanvale St.
Davis, Z. O.	Private	Co. D, 4th Virginia Infantry	948 Milton Place.
Davidson, J. E.	Private	Co. A, Davis Cavalry	1814 Druid Hill Ave.
Davis, Mark N.	Private	Co. D, 13th Virginia Cavalry	1620 Edmondson Ave.
Daue, Wm. M., Rev.	Private	1st Richmond Howitzers	1409 Bolton St.

NAME.	RANK.	BRANCH OF SERVICE.	ADDRESS.
Dardon, George F.	Lieutenant	Co. K, 31st N. C. Infantry	8 Pleasant St.
Davis, John R.	Private	Co. H, 1st Virginia Infantry	M. L. C. S. H.
Davis, Wm. H.	Private	Co. H, 1st Maryland Infantry	M. L. C. S. H.
Davis, James. A.	Lieutenant	Co. F, 2d Maryland Infantry	Linkwood, Dorchester Co., Md.
Davis, Henry B.	Private	Co. K, 1st Virginia Cavalry	Whaleyville, Worcester Co., Md.
DeGournay, P. F.	Lieutenant-Colonel	Artillery, C. S. A.	1121 Druid Hill Ave.
Dement, B. F.	Sergeant-Major	2d Maryland Infantry	Marshall Hall, Charles Co., Md.
Denny, James W.	Private	39th Virginia Cavalry	1900 Linden Ave.
Deppish, Edward C.	Lieutenant	Co. E, 1st Maryland Infantry	909 North Caroline.
Dering, George M.	Assistant Quartermaster	19th Virginia Cavalry	Germantown, Montg'm'y Co. Md.
Delozier, George E.	Private	Co. B, 2d Maryland Infantry	Pisgah, Charles Co., Md.
Dent, H. Clay	Private	Co. B, 2d Maryland Infantry	Issue, Charles Co., Md.
Didlake, Wm. F.	Corp.	Co. B, 26th Virginia Infantry	1358 Garrett Ave.
Dinmock, Wm. C.	Sergeant	Engineer, A. N. V.	2122 St. Paul.
Dittus, J. Fred.	Private	Co. C, 1st Maryland Cavalry	M. L. C. S. H.
Dorsett, J. H.	Private	1st Maryland Artillery	209 South Charles.
Dorsey, Chas. W.	Private	Co. A, 1st Maryland Cavalry	M. L. C. S. H.
Doughty, Wm. E.	Corporal	Co. B, 19th Virginia Artillery	509 N. Calhoun St.
Douglas, H. Kyd	Colonel	General T. J. Jackson's Staff	Hagerstown, Md.
Dornin, Thomas L.	Lieutenant	Confederate States Navy	
Douglas, H. T.	Colonel	Engineers, C. S. A.	1113, N. Charles.
Downing, T. J.	Private	Co. D, 9th Virginia Cavalry	41 Hopkins Place.
Dorsey, Andrew.	Private	Co. A, 1st Maryland Cavalry	Harrisonville, Balto. Co., Md.
Dorsey, Samuel W.	Lieutenant	Co. K, 1st Virginia Cavalry	510 Cathedral.
Doughty, Henry C.	Private	Co. B, 19th Bat. H. Artillery	1214 Mosher St.
Duncan, John J.	Orderly Sergeant	Co. A, Smith's Battalion	1106 W. Lexington.
Dunn, Wm. C.	Captain	Co. E, 37th Virginia Cavalry	Gutman Ave. and Quaker Lane.
Duvall, Tobias.	Private	Co. C, 2d Maryland Infantry	Mitchelsville, Pr. George Co. Md.
Duvall, Daniel	Private	Co. C, 2d Maryland Infantry	Parole, Anne Arundel Co., Md.
Dural, Louis.	Lieutenant	33d Texas Cavalry	M. L. C. S. H.
Duncan, Wm. C.	Private	Turner's Battery	M. L. C. S. H.
Dallom, Charles F.	Private	4th Maryland Artillery	Pennsylvania Ave. and Mosher.
Duval, Frank M.	Private	Co. F, 17th Virginia Infantry	509 Curley St.
Dunnington, C. Allen	Private	Co. A, 4th Virginia Cavalry	114 C St., S.E., Washington, D.C.

NAME.	RANK.	BRANCH OF SERVICE.	ADDRESS.
Duvall, Evans	Private	Co. C, 2d Maryland Infantry	Laurel, Md.
Duvall, Ridgeley	Private	Co. D, 1st Maryland Infantry	1225 Guilford Ave.
Dunahue, Wm.	Private	Co. A, 27th N. C. Infantry	M. L. C. S. H.
Dunlap, D. M.	Private	Co. C, 12th Virginia Infantry	1212 Harlem Ave.
Dudley, Hamilton M	Private	Co. B, 40th Virginia Infantry	Bay Line Steamers.
Dutton, John T.	Private	Co. B, 1st Maryland Cavalry	Tompkinsville, Chas. Co., Md.
Dyser, Luke I	Private	Co. F, 41st Virginia Infantry	Carroll P.O., Baltimore Co., Md.
Dempsey, Joseph	Private	Baltimore Light Artillery	Brooklyn, N. Y.
Duggan, Patrick	Private	Co. B, 7th Virginia Infantry	1802 E. Monument St.
Edell, Henry J	Private	2d Maryland Artillery	1205 Hopkins Ave.
Eisenberg, George	Private	Co. F, 1st Maryland Infantry	15, S. Washington St.
Elder, G. Howard	Private	Co. C, 1st Maryland Cavalry	Pikesville, Md.
Elsesser, Peter	Sergeant	Co. B, 1st S. C. Infantry	Baltimore, Md.
Elliott, J. Wesley	Lieutenant	Co. A, 32d Virginia Infantry	1643 Orleans St.
Ennory, Richard, M. D.	Assistant Surgeon	A. N. V.	Taylor, Md.
Englehardt, Ed. C.	Private	Co. F, 1st Maryland Infantry	1018 Hillen St.
Evans, Dudley	Lieutenant-Colonel	20th Georgia Cavalry	Omaha, Neb.
Exall, Turner P.	Private	Co. G, 3d Virginia Cavalry	129 W. 20th St.
Farley, Richard G	Private	Otey Battery	M. L. C. S. H.
Feast, Loudon	Private	2d Maryland Cavalry	825 W. 25th St., Wash., D. C.
Ferguson, W. I	Private	Co. G, 1st Virginia Infantry	507 N. Gilmor St.
Fenton, Daniel A	Sergeant	Co. G, 2d Maryland Infantry	221 W. Preston St.
Fenton, John J	Sergeant	1st South Carolina Artillery	1207 Argyle Ave.
Fitzgerald, Wm. H	Masters Mate	Confederate States Navy	1811 N. Charles St.
Figg, John Q	Sergeant	Co. B, 1st Virginia Infantry	1110 N. Stricker St.
Flowers, J. W	Private	Co. H, 11th Virginia Infantry	711 Sterling St.
Foley, David R	Private	Co. C, 1st Maryland Cavalry	158 W. West St.
Forbes, J. H.	Captain, A. Q	Andrews' Artillery	Annapolis, Md.
Forrest, Rev. Douglas F	Assistant Quartermaster	Confederate States Navy	Ellicott City, Md
Forsythe, Wm. H.	Private	Co. A, 1st Maryland Cavalry	Sykesville, Md.
Foster, John H.		Mosby's Cavalry	
Foute, Augustus M	Lieutenant-Colonel	General Pemberton's Staff	231 W. Biddle.
Foxwell, Charles J	Private	Co. B, 2d Maryland Infantry	1318 S. Woodvear St.
Franklin, B. E.	Private	Co. H, 3d Virginia Infantry	1821 W. Lombard St.

NAME.	RANK.	BRANCH OF SERVICE.	ADDRESS.
Franklin, Joseph	Private	1st Maryland Artillery	2006 Christian St.
Frederick, Adolph	Private	2d Maryland Artillery	Stillwater, Minn.
Freeman, R. M.	Private	Co. B, 21st Virginia Infantry	St. Clement's Bay, St. Mary's [Co. Md.
Freeman, Bernard	Private	Co. A, 2d Maryland Infantry	113 Commerce St.
Funk, Chas. D	Private	Co. D, 1st Maryland Cavalry	M. L. C. S. H.
Gaither, George R.	Captain	1st Virginia Cavalry	510 Cathedral St.
Gamble, Carey R., M. D	Surgeon	Confederate States Army	925 Cathedral St.
Gardner, Wm. F., Rev.	Chaplain	Pickett's Division	Hooversville, Howard Co., Md.
Garnett, James M.	Captain	Grimes' Division	
Gassette, C. W.	Major	Staff of General Duke	Birmingham, Ala.
Gatch, Thomas B.	Captain	Co. A, Davis Cavalry	Gardenville, Baltimore Co., Md.
Gavan, W. S.	Sergeant	Co. F, 54th Georgia Infantry	718 W. North Ave.
Gallagher, Charles K.	Captain	44th North Carolina Infantry	
Gephart, Sol. A	Private	Co. A, 1st Maryland Cavalry	M. L. C. S. H.
Gibbons, John	Private	2d Maryland Infantry	411 S. Central Ave.
Gibson, Mahlon	Private	1st Virginia Cavalry	
Gill, John	Signal Sergeant	Fitzhugh Lee's Division	929 N. Charles St.
Gill, W. H.	Private	Co. C, 1st Maryland Cavalry	2100 St. Paul St.
Gilmor, Richard T	Lieutenant	2d Maryland Cavalry	M. L. C. S. H.
Gilpin, John	Corporal	1st Maryland Artillery	Elkton, Md.
Gilmor, C. Graham	Sergeant	Co. B, 21st Virginia Infantry	
Glenn, Samuel T	Private	Co. A, 2d Maryland Infantry	Baltimore, Md.
Glocker, A. Campbell	Private	Co. A, 2d Maryland Cavalry	917 N. Gilmor St.
Goldsborough, N. Lee	Private	Co. A, 1st Maryland Infantry	5th Regiment Armory.
Goldsmith, William	Sergeant	54th North Carolina Infantry	M. L. C. S. H.
Goldsborough. W. W.	Major	2d Maryland Infantry	
Goodwin, C. Ridgely	A. D. C.	General Alexander	211 N. Calvert St.
Gorman, W. H.	Private	1st Maryland Artillery	
Gough, Benjamin	Private	Co. I, 4th Virginia Cavalry	M. L. C. S. H.
Grace, Wm.	Private	Co. C, 2d Maryland Infantry	Easton, Talbot Co., Md.
Grady, E. K.	Private	6th Virginia Cavalry	919 Elm St.
Graves, Henry M.	Lieutenant Eng.	Richmond Defences	1215 Madison Ave.
Graves, Wm. B	Sergeant	Utterbach's Battery	109 South St.
Grayson, Spence M.	Private	Co. A, 2d Maryland Infantry	1600 Guilford Ave.

Name.	Rank.	Branch of Service.	Address.
Grant, Richard R.	Lieutenant	Co. D, 5th N. Carolina Infantry.	
Green, Wharton J.	Lieutenant-Colonel	2d North Carolina Battalion	
Greenwell, Joseph A.	Private	2d Maryland Artillery	751 W. Franklin St.
Grimes, Dr. John H.	Private	1st Virginia Cavalry	2100 Maryland Ave.
Grogan, Charles E.	Lieutenant	Mosby's Cavalry	
Grogan, R. Riddle	Lieutenant	1st Maryland Cavalry	
Gross, John	Private	15th Louisiana Regiment	322 Lafayette Ave.
Greenfield, W. H.	Private	Co. G, 1st Maryland Infantry	Baltimore, Md.
Grogan, James J.	Private	Co. C. 1st Maryland Cav.	
Green, Vincent	Private	4th Maryland Artillery	M. L. C. S. H.
Gresham, Thomas B.	Private	Co. B, 2d Georgia Infantry	875 Park Ave.
Green, Louis.	Sergeant.	Co. D, 1st Maryland Infantry	Annapolis, Md.
Green, Matthew	Private.	Co. D, 1st Maryland Infantry	M. L. C. S. H.
Gregory, Oliver F.	Private.	Co. H, 1st Hampton Legion	504 N. Broadway.
Gunderman, Louis.	Musician	Co. D, 1st S. Carolina Artillery	2107, Calverton Road.
Guthric, J. Julius.	Master M	Confederate States Navy	
Gwathney, Robert W.	Private	Otey Battery	Care of Power, Son & Co. N. Y.
Gwyn, John T.	Lieutenant	Co. B, 26th Virginia Infantry	538 N. Arlington Ave.
Hardcastle, A. B.	Colonel	Lowry's Brigade, Army Tenn. Easton. Md.	
Haas, Isaac C.	Private	4th Maryland Artillery	Mt. Washington.
Hager, John H.	Private	Co. C, 1st Maryland Cavalry	Mandan, Dakota.
Haines, John J.	Captain	2d Virginia Infantry	84 S. Howard St.
Hall, James R.	Sergeant.	Co. A, 40th Virginia Infantry	1323 E. Monument St.
Hall, Thomas W., Jr.	Major and I. Gen'l	Department of Alabama, Mississippi and East Louisiana.	16 W. Franklin St.
Hall, Wilburn B.	Lieutenant	Confederate States Navy	310 W. Hoffman St.
Hallman, Martin	Private	Co. K, 13th S. C. Infantry	1314 N. Fremont Ave.
Hammond, John S.	Sergeant.	2d Georgia Cavalry	2036 E. Fayette St.
Hanson, John D.	Sergeant.	Co. I, 1st Maryland Infantry	1105 N. Gilmor St.
Harper, W. H.	Private.	1st Maryland Battery	Upper Malboro, P. G. Co., Md.
Harrison, Thomas D.	Private.	2d Maryland Infantry	400 Courtland St.
Hart, William A.	Corporal.	Otey Battery.	114 W. 22d St.
Hayden, Horace E.	Private.	1st Maryland Cavalry.	Wilkesbarre, Pa.
Hayden, John F.	Private.	Baltimore Light Artillery.	1415 W. Lanvale St.

NAME.	RANK.	BRANCH OF SERVICE.	ADDRESS.
Haynes, Thos. R	Sergeant	Co. K, 55th Virginia Infantry	498 9th St. N. Y.
Haynes, Wm. H	Lieutenant	Co. K, 55th Virginia Infantry	900 N. Fulton Avenue.
Hack, Henry Clav	Sergeant	Co. H, 16th Virginia Infantry	1356 N. Stricker St.
Hawkins, Joseph J	Private	7th N. C. Infantry	M. L. C. S. H.
Hammond, Chas	Private	Co. C, 2nd Maryland Infantry	Baltimore.
Harrison, W. H	Private	Co. C, 2nd Maryland Infantry	400 Courtland St.
Harwood, James K	Paymaster	Confederate States Navy	938 N. Calvert St.
Halbig, J. S	Private	Co. E, 2nd Maryland Infantry	
Hall, Joseph. H	Private	Co. F, 40th Virginia Infantry	1603 Hanover St.
Hayes, Thomas G	Sergeant Major	10th Virginia Cavalry	925 N. Stricker St.
Heath, George R	Sergeant	Co. B, 1st Virginia Infantry	750 W. Saratoga St.
Heimiller, Herman	Private	Co. C, 1st Maryland Cavalry	1428 Light St.
Heimiller, Wm	Private	Co. A, 2nd Maryland Cavalry	1016 N. Central Ave
Heiskell, J. Monroe	Captain	Walker's Battalion	
Herbert, Wm. E	Private	Co. B, 3rd Virginia Infantry	829 Woodward St.
Hewes, James	Private	Co. A, 1st Maryland Infantry	2028 Park Ave.
Heiskell, H. Lee	Captain	Co. G, 2nd Virginia Infantry	M. L. C. S. H.
Henderson, Ladson M	Musician	Co. H, 25th N. C. Infantry	1803 N. Dallas St.
Heinz, Ferd	Musician	Co. C, 23rd Virginia Infantry	M. L. C. S. H.
Heighe, John M	Private	Co. A, 1st Maryland Cavalry	605 N. Charles St.
Hebb, J. Wise, M. D	Assistant Surgeon	7th Louisiana Infantry	Friendship, Howard Co., Md.
Hessee, Edward	Private	Co. K, 48th Virginia Infantry	4 N. Frederick St.
Henry, John C	Private	Co. A, 2nd Maryland Infantry	
Heard, John L	Private	Co. F, 1st Maryland Cavalry	805 N. Caroline St.
Highfield, Thos	Seaman	Confederate States Navy	War Dept., Washington. D. C.
Hill, N. S	Major	A. N. V.	813 N. Charles St.
Hipkins, Richard	Private	Co. G, 6th Virginia Infantry	313 2nd Ave., N. Y.
Higgins, W. G	Private	1st Maryland Artillery	Gambrills, A. A. Co. Md.
Hipsley, Thos	Private	2nd Maryland Cavalry	1808 Dover St.
Hitchcock, Rob't F	Private	Co. B, 1st Virginia Infantry	1328 W. Baltimore St.
Hill, Chas. D	Captain	15th N. C. Infantry	33 S. Gay St.
Hobbs, Wm. H	Musician	2nd Maryland Cavalry	M. L. C. S. H.
Hoblitzell, Fetter S	Private	Co. H, 1st Maryland Infantry	2435 N. Calvert St.
Hoerster, Fred'k	Private	Co. A, 2nd Maryland Infantry	523 Colvin St.

Name.	Rank.	Branch of Service.	Address.
Hoffman, R. Curzen.	Captain	21st Virginia Infantry	1203 St. Paul St.
Hollyday, Geo. T., of G.	Corporal	Co. E, 1st Maryland Cavalry	1048 Hopkins Ave.
Hollyday, Henry	Private	Co. A, 2nd Maryland Infantry	Easton, Talbot Co., Md.
Hollyday, John G., M. D.	Private	Co. C, 1st Maryland Cavalry	714 Frederick Ave.
Hollyday, Lamar	Private	Co. A, 2nd Maryland Infantry	Hygeia Hotel, Old Pt. Comfort.
Holmes, J. C.	Sergeant	2nd Maryland Cavalry	Charlestown, W. Va.
Holmes, James Gadson	Captain	Staff of General Law	119 S. Gay St.
Holtzman, Wm. F	Private	4th Maryland Artillery	542 N. Carey St.
Hough, G.	Private	Mosby's Cavalry	812 St. Paul St.
Hough, Samuel G.	Private	Co. A, 1st Maryland Cavalry	1015 St. Paul St.
Howard, D. Ridgely	Private	Co. A, 2nd Maryland Infantry	939 St. Paul St.
Howard, James	Lieutenant Colonel	18th & 20th Bat. Heavy Artil.	919 Cathedral St.
Howard, John E.	Captain	2nd Maryland Infantry	919 Cathedral St.
Howard, J. McHenry, M. D.	Lieutenant	Staff of Genl. W. H. Stevens.	939 St. Paul St.
Howard, McHenry	Lieutenant	Stonewall Brigade	919 Cathedral St.
Howard, Richard M	Private	Co. C, 1st Maryland Cavalry	Monkton, Balto. Co., Md.
Hobbs, N. Chew	Lieutenant	Co. K, 1st Virginia Cavalry	Cooksville, Howard Co. Md.
Hooper, Rich'd H	Q. M.	Confederate States Navy	
Howell, Charles L.	Landsman	Confederate States Navy	1733 Hollins St.
Hoffman, Geo. W	Private	Co. F, 1st Maryland Infantry	411 N. Bond St.
Hogarthy, Wm	Private	Co. D, 2nd Maryland Infantry	M. L. C. S. H.
Hunter, John J	Private	Co. A, 2nd Maryland Infantry	
Hudgins, Charles H	Lieutenant	Co. E, 24th Virginia Cavalry	15 W. Franklin St.
Hummer, Joseph	Private	Co. F, 1st Maryland Cavalry	M. L. C. S. H.
Hubbard, Alex. J	Musician	1st Maryland Infantry	29 S. Stricker St.
Hunter, Thomas	Private	Co. A, 1st Maryland Cavalry	Wheaton, Montgomery Co., Md.
Hunter, Fred'k, M. D	Assistant Surgeon	1st Maryland Artillery	
Hughes, G. N	Private	Co. K, 17th Virginia Regulars	528 N. Calhoun St.
Hull, Wm. J	Private	5th Virginia Cavalry	1800 N. Calvert St.
Hurt, Henry N	Private	Co. H, 47th Virginia Infantry	668 W. Saratoga St.
Ingraham, Charles H	Private	Co. A, 40th Virginia Infantry	926 N. Calhoun St.
Ingraham, Wm. H	Private	40th Virginia Infantry	116 N. Carey St.
Irvine, J. B	Private	McGregor's Battery	110 Edmondson Ave.
Jacobs, Julius E	Private	Co. H, 6th Virginia Infantry	2032 W. North Ave.

NAME.	RANK.	BRANCH OF SERVICE.	ADDRESS.
Jackson, C. M.	Lieutenant	Co. C, Hood's Battalion	618 Jefferson Ave.
Jarboe, Geo. B.	Private	Co. F, 1st Maryland Cavalry	16 W. Frederick Road.
Jackson, John W.	Private	Purcell Battery	Laurel, Md.
James, Edwin	Quartermaster Sergeant	2nd Maryland Infantry	M. L. C. S. H.
Jenkins, Geo. C.	Private	Co. C, 1st Maryland Cavalry	106 E. Chase St.
Jenkins, Henry	Lieutenant	Wood's Battalion Cavalry	Sykesville, Md.
Jenkins, James W. Jr.	Private	Co. E, 1st Maryland Cavalry	Mt. Washington.
Jenkins, S. Tazwell	Lieutenant	Co. B, 47th Georgia Infantry	124 W. Lanvale St.
Jenkins, W. Kennedy	Private	1st Maryland Artillery	307 E. Lanvale St.
Jennings, B. R.	Private	Co. A, 2nd Maryland Infantry	M. L. C. S. H.
Johnson, Bradley T.	Brigadier General	Maryland Line	Lexington & St. Paul St.
Jobe. R. M.	Private	Co. A, 5th Virginia Infantry	1415 Orleans St.
Johnson, J. W.	Private	Norfolk Light Artillery Blues	1307 W. Mulberry St.
Johnson, O. P.	Captain	Co. F, 32nd Virginia Infantry	Washington, D. C.
Johnson, W. H.	Private	Co. H, 1st Georgia Infantry	621 Columbia Avenue.
Johnston, Bartlett S.	Midshipman	Confederate States Navy	2421 Eutaw Place.
Jones, Albert	Sergeant	Co. D, 1st Maryland Cavalry	Mt. Airy, Md.
Jones, Spencer C.	Private	Co. D, 1st Maryland Cavalry	Rockville, Md.
Jones, Thomas A.	Chief Agent	Secret Service in Maryland	La Platte, Charles Co., Md.
Jones, Geo. W.	Private	Co. H, 18th Virginia Cavalry	M. L. C. S. H.
Keating, James F.	Acting Assistant Surgeon	Washington's Artillery	313 S. Central Ave.
Keats, John T.	Private	1st Maryland Cavalry	Baltimore.
Keeling, John L.	Private	Norfolk Light Artillery Blues	1427 N. Bond St.
Keene, R. Goldsborough	Private	Co. A, 1st Maryland Cavalry	100 East Preston St.
Kellam, Stewart	Private	Co. H, 1st Texas Artillery	Martinsburg, W. Va.
Keesler, J. M.	Private	Co. B, 20th N. C. Infantry	306 N. Carey St.
Kelton, Carlton H.	Private	2nd Maryland Cavalry	Tombstone, Arizona.
Kendall, George E.	Corporal	Latham's Battery	2010 E. Baltimore St.
Kernan, James L.	Private	Baltimore Light Artillery	10 S. Front St.
Kershaw, Edwin	Private	Graham's Battery	211 Carroll St.
Kettlewell, Chas.	Sergeant	Co. C, 1st Maryland Cavalry	204 Spears Wharf.
Kenley, Oliver G.	Private	Co. K, 1st Virginia Cavalry	718 Harford Ave.
Keech, Chilton A.	Private	Co. B, 21st Virginia Infantry	M. L. C. S. H.
Kelly, Francis P.	Private	Pegram's Battery	M. L. C. S. H.

NAME.	RANK.	BRANCH OF SERVICE.	ADDRESS.
King, E. C.	Ordnance Sergeant	17th Virginia Infantry	820 N. Gilmor St.
King, Geo. W.	Private	Herding Department	312 Division St.
King, Thos. S.	Private	Co. E, 55th Virginia Infantry	Bowie, Pr. George Co., Md.
Kinlock, Wm.	Private	Lee Battery	Baltimore.
King, J. C.	Private	Co. B, 15th Louisiana Infantry	534 N. Gilmor St.
King, Wm. John	Private	Co. G, 1st Maryland Infantry	Reisterstown, Md.
Killman, Richard G.	Private	Co. D, 2d Maryland Infantry	Annapolis, Md.
King, Thomson M.	Engineer	Co. G, 7th Virginia Cavalry	Obligation, A. A. Co., Md.
Kirkland, Ed. P.	Surgeon	Confederate States Navy	M. L. C. S. H.
Kloman, Wm. C., M. D.	Surgeon	Confederate States Army	804 North Ave.
Kloman, E. F.	Private	Mosby's Cavalry	
Knight, John J.	Sergeant	Co. F, 5th Virginia Cavalry	228 Warren Ave.
Knight, Dr., Louis W.	Private	2d Maryland Artillery	414 N. Greene St.
Knox, Richard T.	Sergeant	Co. C, 1st Maryland Cavalry	224 S. Collington Ave.
Kneller, Jacob S.	Private	Co. D, 1st Maryland Infantry	330 N. Stricker St.
Krause, Chas. H.	Private	Co. E, 1st Maryland Cavalry	Goldsboro, N. C.
Krener, Fred. M.	Private	Co. A, 2d Maryland Cavalry	400 W. Camden St.
Lackland, Wm.	Sergeant	Co. E, 6th Louisiana Infantry	M. L. C. S. H.
Laird, Wm. H.	Private	Co. A, 2d Maryland Infantry	Brookville, Md.
Lamates, James	Sergeant	1st Maryland Infantry	304 E. Fort Ave.
Landsreet, E.	Private	Co. A, 1st Virginia Cavalry	Memphis, Tenn.
Latimer, Thos. S., M. D.	Surgeon	A. N. V.	103 W. Monument St.
Latrobe, Osmun	Lieutenant Colonel	1st Corps A. N. V.	1205 St. Paul St.
Latrobe, R. Steuart	Private	Co. C, 1st Maryland Cavalry	14 E. Eager St.
Laughter, Wm. H.	Lieutenant	18th Virginia Battery Artillery	302 W. Lanvale St.
Lawson, Campbell G.	Captain	Co. H, 15th Virginia Infantry	Clk Bay View.
Lawson, W. M.	Captain	1st Virginia Infantry	Lee Camp Soldier's Home.
Lee, Humphrey, W.	Sergeant	32d Virginia Infantry	620 Clinton Ave.
Lee, I. Boykin	Ordnance Sergeant	7th South Carolina Cavalry	1300 N. Charles St.
Lee, Wills.	Private	2nd Co. Richmond Howitzers	St. Paul and Fayette St.
Legg, Edgar K.	Private	Co. H, 13th Virginia Infantry	2103 Oak St.
Lepper, Chas. V.	Private	Co. K, 1st Virginia Cavalry	Philadelphia, Pa.
Lee, Otho S.	Sergeant Major	Steuart's Horse Artillery	Bel Air, Md.
Lee, Juo Mason	Major	Staff Fitzhugh Lee	

NAME.	RANK.	BRANCH OF SERVICE.	ADDRESS.
Lee, Daniel Murray	Passed-Midshipman	Confederate States Navy	•
Leutbecher, Chas.	Private	Co. A, 19th Virginia Infantry	422 S. Paca St.
Leonard, Michael J.	Private	Co. G, 1st Maryland Infantry	1041 Hollins St.
Lewis, Jno. Wm.	Sergeant	Co. I, 8th Virginia Cavalry	611 W. Madison St.
Leigh, John H.	Private	Co. A, 5th Virginia Cavalry	245 W. Preston St.
Lee, Chas. W.	Private	1st Maryland Infantry	Aberdeen, Md.
Lickle, John D., M. D.	Private	Co. D, 1st Maryland Cavalry	810 N. Fulton Ave.
Livesay, James A.	Private	Co. E, 3rd Virginia Infantry	109 S. Fulton Ave.
Linzay, James H.	Private	Co. C, 1st Maryland Cavalry	Towson, Balto. Co., Md.
Livesay, T. T.	Sergeant	3rd Virginia Infantry	303 S. Fulton Ave.
Loimax, William R.	Private	Co. K, 5th Virginia Cavalry	116 N. Paca St.
Long, Patrick	Private	Co. A, 60th Virginia Infantry	1522 Hampstead St.
Lorsch, Henry	Private	Co. A, 19th Virginia Infantry	Baltimore,
Lowe, Wm. Edwin	Private	Co. A, 2d Maryland Infantry	McDanielstown, Talbot Co., Md.
Loveday, Carl L.	Private	Co. F, 12th Virginia Cavalry	M. L. C. S. H.
Lowe, Wm. L.	Private	Co. A, 2d Maryland Infantry	Centreville. Md.
Lucchesi, David H.	Private	Co. A, 2d Maryland Infantry	2268 McCulloh St.
Lurman, G. W.	Private	Co. C, 1st Maryland Cavalry	10 South St.
Lunsden, D. L.	Private	Co. H, 2d S. C. Cavalry	M. L. C. S. H.
Lyon, James W.	Major	Confederate States Army	New Orleans, La.
Lyell, Henry	Private	Co. K, 9th Virginia Cavalry	726 N. Carey St.
Lyle, Duncan C.	Lieutenant	4th Virginia Reserves	McDonough Institute.
Macatee, Ig. J.	Private	Co. C, 1st Maryland Cavalry	Pylesville, Md.
Macgill, Chas. G. W., M. D.	Surgeon	2d Virginia Cavalry	Catonsville. Balto. Co., Md.
Mackall, Thos. B.	Lieutenant, A. D. C.	Staff of Gen. W. W. Mackall	149 W. Lanvale St.
Machen, T. H.	Private	Co. F, 5th Virginia Cavalry	802 N. Gilmor St.
Mackubbin, Clarence H.	Private	Co. K, 1st Virginia Cavalry	1434 Decatur St.
Maguire, Geo. W.	Private	Co. A, 1st Maryland Infantry	Washington, D. C.
Mahoney, John	Private	Co. G, 1st S. C. H. Artillery	M. L. C. S. H.
maitbie, J. R.	Private	4th Tennessee Infantry	101 W. Lexington St.
Maloy, Rev. Wm. C.	Chaplain	44th Miss. Regiment	1027 McCulloh St.
Manly, Gaston	Sergeant Major	Manly's Artillery	Ellicott City.
Manning, Richard I.	Major, A. D. C.	Staff of Gen. Jos. E. Johnston	Stansburg, S. C.
Marck, Allen L.	Private	Defences of Petersburg	1439 Park Ave.

NAME.	RANK.	BRANCH OF SERVICE.	ADDRESS.
Marck, W. B.	Sergeant	30th Virginia Infantry	817 N. Gilmor St.
Markoe, Frank	Lieutenant and Ord. Officer	Gen. J. B. Gordon's Division	7 N. Calvert St.
Marney, John	Ord.-Sergeant	1st Maryland Infantry	607 Roland Ave.
Marshall, Charles	Lieutenant Colonel	Staff of Gen. R. E. Lee	1209 St. Paul St.
Martin, James	Private	Co. C, 5th Virginia Cavalry	956 Franklin Road
Martin, Thomas B	Private	Co. F, 24th Virginia Cavalry	757 Ramsey St.
Marye, J. L.	Sergeant	Fredericksburg Battery	409 St. Paul St.
Marchant, A. W.	Private	Co E, 5th Virginia Cavalry	1617 N. Calhoun St.
Martindale, Henry H	Private	Co. K, 14th N. C. Infantry	411 N. Calhoun St.
Maslin, J. M.	Private	7th Virginia Cavalry	1611 Bolton St.
Mason, John T. of R.	Passed-Midship	Confederate States Navy	808 N. Fremont St.
Mason, Thomas P.	Private	26th Virginia Infantry	1019 N. Stricker St.
Mason, A. S.	Surgeon	A. N. V.	Hagerstown, Md.
Masson, Geo. F.	Sergeant	Co. F, 5th Virginia Cavalry	854½ W. Lombard St.
Massenberg, R. C.	Lieutenant and Adjutant	Findlay's Batalion	Towson, Balto. Co., Md.
Mattison, Samuel J.	Ord.-Sergeant	Baltimore Light Artillery	1716 Mosher St.
Matthews, Albert E.	Captain	Co. H. 8th Virginia Infantry	11 E. Hoffman St.
Maxwell, James A	Private	Maxwell Light Artillery	Boston, Mass.
Maynadier, J. H.	Private	Co. K, 1st Virginia Cavalry	211 W. Preston St.
McAvoy, Joseph V	Private	22d Miss. Infantry	M. L. C. S. H.
McAlwee, Geo. W	Corporal	2d Maryland Artillery	Richmond, Va.
McAleer, Joseph L	Captain	Co. D, 2d Maryland Infantry	Ysleta, Texas.
McBlair, Wm	Master Mate	Confederate States Navy	Washington, D. C.
McCann, Charles	Lieutenant	Pryor's Brigade	1706 Harlem Ave.
McCann, Wm. V	Private	Co. C, 2d Maryland Infantry	M. L. C. S. H.
McCardell, Thomas F.	Lieutenant	Co. C, 64th Virginia Infantry	Eckart, Allegheny Co., Md.
McCawley, Wm. N.	Lieutenant	Co. K, 9th Virginia Cavalry	433 Conway St.
McClure, G. D.	Private	Chesapeake Artillery	1541 W. North Ave.
McCreery, J. V. L.	Sergeant	1st Richmond Howitzer's	Hanover C. H., Va.
Macculibin, R. W., Jr	Private	Baltimore Light Artillery	660 W. Baltimore St.
McCauley, Daniel	Private	Staunton Hill Artillery	M. L. C. S. H.
McCullough, S. Thomas	Lieutenant	Co. D, 2d Maryland Infantry	2 Maryland Ave.
McClure, James N	Sergeant	Co. D, 6th Virginia Cavalry	M. L. C. S. H.
McDonald, Patrick	Private	Co. A, 2d Maryland Infantry	3141 Elliott St.

NAME.	RANK.	BRANCH OF SERVICE.	ADDRESS.
McEntee, James J	Private	Co. G, 2nd Maryland Infantry.	817 Columbia Ave.
McGee, George R	Private	Co. B, 21st Virginia Infantry.	Bolton near Boundary.
McGlone, Bernard F		1st Maryland Artillery.	Timonium.
McIntosh, D. G.	Colonel.	McIntosh Artillery.	Towson, Balto. Co., Md.
McKenna, Patrick J	Private	1st Virginia Infantry	741 W. Lombard St.
McKenna, Peter	Private	Co. E, Stewart's Artillery	104 Scott St.
McKevitt, Arthur	Private	Co. F, 1st Maryland Infantry.	411 E. Monument St.
McKnew, W. R., M. D.	Assistant Surgeon	1st Maryland Cavalry.	1401 Linden Ave.
McKelvey, Charles M	Sergeant	Co. D, 36th Virginia Cavalry.	1200 N. Gay St.
McKim, Rev., Randolph H.	A. D. C.	Gen. George H. Steuart	Washington, D. C.
McLaughlin, Frank	Private	Co. G, 15th Virginia Infantry.	M. L. C. S. H.
McLanahan, W. H.	Private	Co. D, 1st Maryland Cavalry	
McLaurin, Geo. W	Private	Co. E, 4th Virginia Cavalry	1014 Hopkins Ave.
McNulty, John R	1st Lieutenant	Baltimore Light Artillery	99 Wall St., N. Y.
McWilliams, John	Sergeant Major	15th Virginia Infantry	2218 N. Calvert St.
McWilliams, Frank	Private	1st Maryland Infantry	110 St. Paul St.
McWilliams, Hugh	Private	Co. C, 1st Maryland Cavalry.	223 Warren Ave.
McQueen, Andrew M	Private	Co. G, 25 N. C. Infantry	453 W. 5th St.
Mauphin, Chapman	Lieutenant	1st Regiment Engineer, A. N. V.	Ellicott City, Md.
Meehan, C. J	Private	Co. H, 8th Louisiana Infantry	Elysville, Md.
Melvin, George F	Private	Gen. Elzey's Command.	602 Scott St.
Mettee, C. H	Private	Chesapeake Artillery	1857 E. Biddle St.
Miles, F. T., M. D.	Captain	Co. A, 27th S. C. Infantry	514 Cathedral St.
Miles, A. R	Private	9th Virginia Cavalry	802 Harlem Ave.
Millan, George S.	Private	Co. D, 17th Virginia Infantry	
Minor, G. C.	Sergeant	Co. D, 55th Virginia Volunteers.	1007 N. Mount St.
Miller, Joel	Colonel	Gen. Price, Mo. Army	Austin, Texas.
Mitchell, T. Halcombe.	Private	Co. A, 11th Virginia Infantry.	Towson, Balto. Co., Md.
Morfit, Mason.	Major	Confederate States Army	143 W. Lafayette Ave.
Morgan, W. L., M. D.	Sergeant	Co. A, 51st Virginia Infantry.	202 W. Franklin St.
Morgan, Wm. T	Corporal	Co. A, Armistead's Artillery	420 Conway St.
Morris, C. M.	Lieutenant Commander	C. S. Steamer Florida	220 Charles St. Ave.
Morgan, B. H.	Lieutenant	Co. K, 1st Virginia Cavalry	1009 Harlem Ave.
Monahan, James J	Private	2d Maryland Artillery	1722 Harlem Ave.

NAME.	RANK.	BRANCH OF SERVICE.	ADDRESS.
Mordecai, J. Randolph	Captain	Artillery A. N. V.	Lutherville, Md.
Morton, Richard	Colonel	Nitre and Mining Bureau	213 W. Lanvale St.
Moughan, Patrick	Private	Co. F, 15th Virginia Infantry	2139 Division St.
Muhly, Chas. W.	Private	6th South Carolina Cavalry	28 E. Randall St.
Mullen, Chas. X.	Private	Co. G, 1st So. Car. Infantry	M. L. C. S. H.
Mullikin, Beale D.	Corporal	Co. C, 2nd Maryland Infantry	Halls, Prince George's Co., Md.
Mumford, Henry A.	Corporal	Co. G, 2nd Maryland Infantry	
Mumford William	Lieutenant-Colonel	Confederate States Army	Fair Lee, Kent Co., Md.
Murkland, W. U., Rev.	Sergeant-Major	20th Virginia Regiment	502 Cathedral St.
Moeller, George H.	Private	Co. H, 10th Virginia Cavalry	Mt. Winans, Baltimore.
Monnonier, John N., M. D.	Surgeon	Confederate States Army	824 N. Calvert St.
Moog, James R.	Private	Co. B, 1st Maryland Infantry	1349 N. Gilmor St.
Murphy, J. F.	Ordnance Sergeant	1st South Carolina Infantry	220 S. Bond St.
Murray, Clapham	Lieutenant	Co. A, 2nd Maryland Infantry	13 E. Lafayette Ave.
Murray, Stirling	Sergeant	Stewart's Artillery	Leesburg, Va.
Murray, James	Sergeant	Co. F, 6th Louisiana Infantry	904 Brevard St.
Murray, Alex.	Private	Co. A, 2nd Maryland Infantry	West River, A. A. Co., Md.
Muse, Samuel W.	Private	Co. E, 5th Virginia Cavalry	502 N. Arlington Ave.
Moylan, Wm.	Private	Co. C, 32nd Virginia Infantry	5 Mott St.
Myrick, John T.	Private	Co. K, 34th Virginia Infantry	1108 S. Patuxent St.
Mullen, Joseph, Jr.	Corporal	Co. F, 27th No. Car. Infantry	1421 Bolton St.
Nash, Wadsworth	Private	Norfolk Light Artillery Blues.	118 South St.
Neale, Augustus W.	Private	Co. B, 2nd Maryland Infantry	Spring Hill, Charles Co., Md.
Nelson, Francis F.	Private	1st Maryland Artillery	508 W. Biddle St.
Nicholas, Wilson C.	Captain	Co. G, 1st Maryland Infantry	Owings Mills, Balto. Co., Md.
Nightingale, John A.	Private	Co. H, 17th Virginia Infantry	Alexandria, Va.
Nock, George S.	Private	Co. F, 46th Virginia Infantry	104 Milton Place.
Noland, George W.	Sergeant	Co. A, 2nd Virginia Infantry	623 W. Mulberry St.
Nolley, M. J.	Sergeant	Co. G, 31st No. Car. Infantry	428 N. Carey St.
Norris, William	Colonel	Chief Signal Corps & S. S. Bu.	Reisterstown, Balto. Co., Md.
Northrop, Lucien B.	Brigadier-General	Commissary General, C. S. A.	M. L. C. S. H.
Nutt, James M.	Private	40th Virginia Infantry	34 S. Schroeder St.
Obenderfer, Augustus	Private	Co. F, 2nd Maryland Infantry	Frederick, Md.
Obendorf, A., Jr.	Private	10th Alabama Infantry	1508 McCulloh St.

NAME.	RANK.	BRANCH OF SERVICE.	ADDRESS.
O'Donovan, Edward	Private	Co. A, 2nd Maryland Infantry	Sweet Air, Baltimore Co.
O'Leary, Jerome	Private	Co. D, 1st Maryland Cavalry	Chesterfield, A. A. Co., Md.
Oliver, Wm. H.	Private	Co. F, 5th Virginia Cavalry	1143 Argyle Ave.
Opie, Thos., M. D.	Assistant Surgeon	Confederate States Army	600 N. Howard St.
Otey, K.	Colonel	11th Virginia Infantry	Richmond, Va.
Ott, George M.	Private	Co. D, 1st Maryland Cavalry	Frederick, Md.
Owen, Wyatt	Private	Co. E, 3d Texas Cavalry	Equit. Bldg. Calvert & Fayette
Owens, James W.	Corporal	1st Maryland Battery	Lothain, A. A. Co., Md.
Owens, R. W.	Private	1st Maryland Battery	815 N. Stricker St.
Owens, W. H.	Private	Co. C, Lucas Battalion	30 William St.
Paca, F. T.	Private	Co. E, 1st Maryland Cavalry	Carmichael, Q. A. Co., Md.
Packard, Joseph, Jr.	Lieutenant	Ord. Dep't, A. N. V.	806 St. Paul St.
Page, Dr. I. R.	Surgeon	10th Virginia Infantry	1266 Linden Ave.
Page, Wm.	Private	Co. D, 2d Maryland Infantry	Mill Park, Charles Co., Md.
Palmer, A. J.	Private	Co. C, 1st Maryland Cavalry	405 N. Paca St.
Parker, G. S.	Private	Co. B, 1st Maryland Cavalry	Barboursville, Va.
Parr, D. Preston, Jr.	Private	Co. A, 1st Maryland Infantry	202 Bowly's Wharf.
Patterson, Francis W., M. D.	Surgeon	A. N. V.	Lochearn, Balto. Co., Md.
Pearson, James F.	Sergeant	Co. A, 2nd Maryland Infantry	334 Pressman St.
Pearman, W. C.	Private	Co. G, 15th Virginia Regulars	1133 W. Lombard St.
Pendleton, David E.	Private	Co. A, 7th Virginia Cavalry	832 W. Lombard St.
Pease, Charles C	Private	1st Maryland Artillery	617 George St.
Pendergrass, Charles.	Drummer	Co. C, Wheat's Battalion	M. L. C. S. H.
Perrin, John T.	Captain	Co. E, 26th Virginia Infantry	2022 Maryland Ave.
Perry, John, Jr.	Private	Co. E, 15th Virginia Infantry	1418 W. Franklin St.
Perry, Wm. F.	Private	Co. H, 1st Maryland Infantry	Great Mills, St. Mary's Co., Md.
Perdue, John	Private	Co. A, 1st Maryland Cavalry	Monkton, Balto. Co., Md.
Perrival, C. D.	Private	Co. G, 11th Virginia Infantry	1613 E. Oliver St.
Peterkin, Rt. Rev. George W	Lieutenant	Staff of Gen. Pendleton	Parkersburg, W. Va.
Peters, Winfield	Lieutenant	Richmond Defenses	1117 McCulloh St.
Pettitt, Allen O.	Private	2nd Maryland Cavalry	20 Philadelphia Road.
Pierce, William M.	Private	Co. B, Maury's Battalion	114 Ashland Ave.
Pilker, Michael	Private	Co. G, 1st Maryland Infantry	1020 Watson St.
Pinkney, Wm. S.	Private	Co. H, 1st Maryland Infantry	227 N. Calvert St.

Name.	Rank.	Branch of Service.	Address.
Pippin, E. A.	Sergeant	Co. D, 42nd Virginia Cavalry	1002 Hopkins Ave.
Pittman, A. J.	Private	Co. D, 67th N. C. Infantry	721 W. Pratt St.
Poe, John A.	Private	Co. E, 20th Virginia Infantry	5 W. West St.
Plantz, Geo. W.	Private	Co. K, 15th Virginia Infantry	356 N. Calvert St.
Poe, Neilson, Jr.	Engineer	Confederate States Army	146 W. Lexington St.
Poindexter, Rev. J. Edward	Captain	Co. H, 38th Virginia Infantry	Port Tobacco, Charles Co., Md.
Pollard, C. R.	Sergeant-Major	30th Virginia Infantry	1404 Argyle Ave.
Polk, Trusten	Private	Co. A, 1st Maryland Cavalry	Sykesville, Md.
Poor, Richard L.	Major	Corps Eng, A. N. V.	922 Cathedral St.
Pope, William H	Sergeant	Co. A, 1st Maryland Infantry	511 N. Schroeder St.
Porter, Robert T	Private	Norfolk Light Artillery Blues	630 Clinton Ave.
Powell, R. M.	Colonel	General Hood's Brigade	St. Louis, Mo.
Powell, Edward B.	Captain	Co. F, 6th Virginia Cavalry	41 S. Holliday St.
Powell, Alfred H.	Surgeon	A. N. V.	212 W. Madison St.
Price, Orlando K.	Private	Co. E, 3rd Virginia Infantry	914 N. Gilmor St.
Prince, Lawrence L.	Private	Inglis Light Battery	St. Louis, Mo.
Probest, George E.	Sergeant	2nd Maryland Infantry	715 Edmondson Ave.
Pullen, John F.	Sergeant	Co. G, 5th Virginia Cavalry	Govanstown, Md.
Pumphrey, Lemuel	Sergeant	6th Virginia Infantry	1737 Oliver St.
Purnell, George W	Lieutenant	Co. B, Gilmor's Cavalry	Snow Hill, Md.
Pyfer, Henry	Private	Co. A, 2nd Maryland Infantry	
Pyne, James F	Private	5th Virginia Infantry	1034 W. Fayette St.
Quinn, R. M.	Captain	Confederate States Army	Mobile, Ala.
Raddatz, Chas. F.	Lieutenant	Ord. Dept., E. K. Kirby	Imperial Hotel.
Ramsay, H. Ashton	Lieutenant-Colonel	Confederate States Army	1703 St. Paul St.
Ramsey, W. S.	Lieutenant	61st No. Car. Infantry	515 N. Carey St.
Ramson, A. R. H	Major	O. D, A. N. V.	3 E. Preston St.
Rasin, Maccall M.	Lieutenant	Moore's Artillery	Worten, Kent Co., Md.
Rasin, Wm. I.	Captain	Co. E, 1st Maryland Cavalry	859 Park Avenue.
Rea, George A.	Private	Co. H, 1st Virginia Infantry	795 N. Mount St.
Reary, William A.	Private	Co. K, 6th Virginia Infantry	505 N. Arlington Ave.
Reardon, L. M.	Private	Mosby's Cavalry	518 N. Eutaw St.
Redwood, Allen C.	Private	Co. C, 1st Maryland Cavalry	New York City.
Reilley, John H. F.	Private	Co. B, 1st Maryland Cavalry	Light St. near Hamburg.

NAME.	RANK.	BRANCH OF SERVICE.	ADDRESS.
Reilly, John T	Private	Co. C, 1st Maryland Cavalry	1415 W. Saratoga St.
Reister, P. P.	Private	Co. F, 39th Virginia Infantry	1073 W. Fayette St.
Rider, Martin L. S.	Private	Co. A, 2d Maryland Infantry	Jeffersonton, Va.
Rich, Rev. E. R.	Corporal	Co. E, 1st Maryland Cavalry	Orleisonia, Pa.
Richardson, R. T.	Private	1st Maryland Artillery	623 N. Carrollton Ave.
Richardson, Shepard D	Lieutenant	26th Virginia Regiment	234 E. Montgomery St.
Richardson, S. H.	Lieutenant	Co. B, 53d Virginia Infantry	900 N. Fulton St.
Ridgley, Samuel	Private	1st Maryland Cavalry	Cumberland, Md.
Riley, John	Private	Co. G, 5th Louisiana Infantry	M. L. C. S. H.
Robertson, D., Jr.	Lieutenant	Co. G, 6th Virginia Infantry	32 S. Calvert St.
Ritter, William L	Captain	Ritter's Light Artillery	541 N. Carrollton Ave.
Robinson, George S.	Private	Baltimore Light Artillery	912 N. Arlington Ave.
Robinson, Monroe	Private	Mosby's Cavalry	2030 Maryland Ave.
Robertson, William C	Lieutenant	Co. H, 55th Virginia Infantry	217 South St.
Robinson, Logan	Private	Home Guards	1026 W. Franklin St.
Roberts, Ed.	Private	Co. E, 1st Maryland Infantry	Easton, Md.
Rhodes, W. Lee	Captain	8th Georgia Cavalry	Greencastle, Pa
Rhodes, Oliver L.	Private	McNeal's Rangers	233 W. Lanvale St.
Riordan, John D.	Private	Wise Artillery	820 St. Peter St.
Roe, Samuel	Corporal	Co. E, 1st Maryland Cavalry	Centreville, Md.
Roberts, John T.	Private	Fredericksburg Artillery	2016 Division St.
Rodgers, John M.	Private	Co. H, 12th Virginia Infantry	605 George St.
Roll, John	Private	Co. C, 19th Mississippi Inf'y	M. L. C. S. H.
Rolph, George W	Private	Co. E, 1st Maryland Cavalry	2134 Oak St.
Roper, James M	Ord. Sergeant	Co. I, 6th Virginia Infantry	408 Camden St.
Ryan, Robert S.	Private	Co. D, 1st Maryland Infantry	918 Ashland Ave.
Ryan, James A.	Private	Co. H, 1st Maryland Infantry	1532 W. Fayette St.
Rye, John S.	Sergeant	Co. I, 6th Virginia Infantry	931 Hillen St.
Ryland, Samuel P., Jr	Private	Co. K, 34th Virginia Infantry	15 E. Eager St.
Sadler, D. M.	Private	Co. C, 11th Texas Cavalry	918 N. Arlington Av.
Sakers, John T.	Private	1st Maryland Cavalry	Laurel, Md.
Sanford, R. A.	Private	Co. C, 9th Virginia Cavalry	920 N. Caroline St.
Sanders, T. Hillen	Private	Co. L, 1st Virginia Cavalry	
Sargeant, H. D. G. C.	Private	1st Maryland Artillery	865 N. Howard St.

NAME.	RANK.	BRANCH OF SERVICE.	ADDRESS.
Saunders, John S.	Lieutenant-Colonel.	Ord. Department.	129 W. Leavale St.
Savage, George.	Private.	Otey Battery.	412 Cathedral St.
Savage, Wm. H.	Master's Mate.	C. S. Steamer Stonewall.	1906 Christain St.
Schafer, George Wm.	Private.	Gilmor's Cavalry.	1604 E. Madison St.
Scharf, J. Thomas.	Midshipman.	Confederate States Navy.	1624 Linden Ave.
Schultz, Henry.	Sergeant.	Co. D, 1st S. Carolina Infantry.	M. L. C. S. H.
Scott, John W.	Sergeant.	Co. B, 21st Virginia Infantry.	1731 Guilford Ave.
Selden, Robert T.	Lieutenant.	P. A. C. S.	1018 St. Paul St.
Semmes, Charles W.	Orderly Sergeant.	Letcher Battery.	M. L. C. S. H.
Severe, Francis.	Private.	12th Alabama Regiment.	1718 I. Baltimore St.
Shandley, Patrick.	Private.	Co. I, 20th Georgia Infantry.	
Shanks, Morris.	Private.	Steuart's Horse Artillery.	1130 Argyle Ave.
Shanley, Thomas E.	Private.	Co. A, 2d Maryland Infantry.	214 W. Conway St.
Shepherd, Henry E.	Captain.	43d North Carolina Infantry.	
Shriver, A. K.	Lieutenant.	Richmond Defence.	106 W. Saratoga St.
Shriver, Mark O.	Private.	Co. K, 1st Maryland Cavalry.	607 St. Paul St.
Shriver, Thomas Herbert.	Private.	Va. Military Institute Cadets.	226 St. Paul St.
Shriver, C. C.	Sergeant.	Co. I, 3d Virginia Infantry.	1319 No. Calvert St.
Simon August.	Private.	Co. D, 1st Maryland Infantry.	268 N. Howard St.
Simmons, Daniel S.	Private.	Co. I, 4th N. C. Infantry.	
Sinclair, W. B., M. D.	Surgeon.	Confederate States America.	920 Cathedral St.
Skaggs, E. C.	Private.	Co. K, 14th Virginia Cavalry.	Lewisburg, West Virginia.
Skidmore, William S.	Private.	Co. A, 9th Virginia Cavalry.	406 N. Pine St.
Skinner, Charles W.	Midshipman.	Confederate States Navy.	Washington, D. C.
Skinner, F. G.	Colonel.	1st Virginia Infantry.	New York.
Slater, John H.	Private.	Co. A, 46th Virginia Infantry.	160 Madison Ave. Extension.
Slingluff, Fielder C.	Lieutenant.	1st Maryland Cavalry.	1211 N. Calvert St.
Small, Charles W.	Private.	Co. D, 1st Maryland Infantry.	2015 Maryland Ave.
Smith, Andrew J.	Private.	1st South Carolina Artillery.	113 Scott St.
Smith, Augustine J.	Captain.	31st Virginia Infantry.	428 Mulberry St.
Smith, John Dowell.	Captain.	Battery A, Hugess Battalion.	505 Park Ave.
Smith, R. Carter.	Lieutenant-Colonel.	Commanding Prison, Danville.	5 E. Lexington.
Smith, Thomas B.	Private.	Co. A, 7th Virginia Cavalry.	1303 W. North Ave.
Smith, Victor.	Lieutenant.	Engineer Corps.	22 Mt. Vernon Place.

NAME.	RANK.	BRANCH OF SERVICE.	ADDRESS.
Smith, Walter G.	Private	Steuart's Horse Artillery	1507 Linden Ave.
Smith, Frederick	Captain	Nitre and Mining Corps	1004 Cathedral St.
Smith, Simeon	Private	Co. K. 4th N. C. Infantry	Baltimore.
Smith, Samuel P.	Corporal	Baltimore Heavy Artillery	M. L. C. S. H.
Smith, George H.	Private	Co. F, 25th Virginia Infantry	St. Mary's County, Md.
Smith, W. S.	Private	Co. K, 2d Maryland Infantry	Oriole, Somerset Co., Md.
Snead, S. Wesley	Private	Co. K, 13th Virginia Cavalry	522 N. Paca St.
Snowden, DeWilton, M. D.	Assistant Surgeon	2d Maryland Infantry	Laurel, Md.
Snowden, John C.	Private	Co. C, 1st Maryland Cavalry	515 W. Mulberry St.
Sojecki, Isadore S.	Private	Gilmor's Battalion	Cinneh Home.
Sollers, Somervel	Private	Co. A, 2d Maryland Infantry	1309 John St.
Solomon, Samuel L.	M. Arms	Co. D, 1st Maryland Cavalry	1512 E. Baltimore St.
Sothoron, M. L.	P. Master	1st Maryland Artillery	224 Burk St.
Southerd, Hugh	Private	Co. A, 30th Virginia Infantry	Charlotte Hall, St. Mary's Co... [Md.
Southworth, Clinton	Lieutenant	Fredericksburg Artillery	M. L. C. S. H.
Spedden, John R.	Private	2d Maryland Cavalry	1405 E. Pratt St.
Spencer, E. N.	Private	Co. B, 21st Virginia Infantry	Baltimore.
Spencer, Jervis, Jr.	Private	Co. C, 1st Maryland Cavalry	14 Donnell Building, Baltimore.
Stanley, L. H.	Private	Co. B, 1st Maryland Cavalry	400 Equitable Building.
Staub, Richard P. H.	Captain	Confederate States Army	1407 Linden Ave.
Staylor, Charles H.	Private	Co. E, 5th Louisiana Infantry	925 Elm Place.
Stevenson, D. H.	Private	Co. D, 1st Maryland Cavalry	823 N. Arlington Ave.
Stevenson, Charles E.	Captain	8th Virginia Cavalry	416 W. Fayette St.
Steuart, George H.	Brigadier General	Maryland Line	Carrollton Hotel.
Stewart, C. J.	Private	Gilmor's Battalion	7 S. Liberty St.
Stewart, W. E.	Major	15th Arkansas Infantry	Easton, Md.
Steele, Billings	Private	43d Virginia Infantry	Annapolis, Md.
Stinchcomb, Joshua E.	Private	1st Maryland Artillery	642 W. Lee St.
Stine, Joseph A.	Sergeant	2d Maryland Cavalry	253 S. Bond St.
Stinson, Rober J.	Private	Baltimore Light Artillery	515 W. Lafayette Ave.
Stocksdale. F. G.	Private	Co. C, 2d Maryland Cavalry	749 N. Fulton Ave.
Stonebraker, Joseph R.	Private	Co. C, 1st Maryland Cavalry	1921 Eutaw Place.
Strahan, Charles	Lieutenant	A. N. V.	Cottage City, Mass.

NAME.	RANK.	BRANCH OF SERVICE.	ADDRESS.
Strasburg, D. E.	Musician	Stonewall Brigade	632 W. Lombard.
Street, John H.	Private	Co. A, 1st Maryland Infantry	2234 McCulloh St.
Stringer, Thomas C.	Sergeant	Co. I, 5th Virginia Infantry	1402 W. Lanvale St.
Stubbs, Daniel W.	Lieutenant	Co. G, 18th Tennessee Infantry	811 Hanover St.
Sullivan, Clement	Lieutenant-Colonel	Staff of Gen. G. W. C. Lee	Cambridge, Md.
Sullivan, Frank	Private	Co. C, 1st Maryland Cavalry	1728 N. Calvert St.
Surratt, John H.	Messenger	Secret Service Bureau	1825 Edmondson Ave.
Surratt, Isaac D.	Private	33d Texas Cavalry	407 St. Paul St.
Sutton, John C.	Private	Richmond Fayette Artillery	Richmond, Va.
Sydnor, A. J.	Captain	Co. B, 40th Virginia Infantry	M. L. C. S. H.
Symington, Thomas A.	Captain and A. C. G.	Dearing's Brigade	Catonsville, Md.
Symington, W. Steuart	Major	Staff of Gen. Geo. E. Pickett	615 Park Ave.
Sweeting, B. F.	Private	Co. F, 1st Maryland Cav.	M. L. C. S. H.
Syntis, Sylvester	Private	Co. A, 18th Georgia Battalion	1537 Myrtle Ave.
Tabb, John	Private	Cadets, Va. Military Institute	1724 N. Charles St.
Talbott, J. Fred C.	Private	Co. F, 2d Maryland Cavalry	Lutherville, Md.
Taliaferro, Garvin C.	Adjutant	9th Virginia Cavalry	111 W. Mulberry.
Tanera, Frank	Private	Co. H, 47th Virginia Infantry	Baltimore.
Taylor, David B.	Private	15th Virginia Cavalry	27 S. Howard St.
Taylor, Algernon S.	Colonel	Confederate States M. Corps	M. L. C. S. H.
Tayloe, John	Lieutenant	Cadets, Va. Military Institute	
Tearney, Leonidas	Private	Co. B, 12th Virginia Cavalry	Cumberland.
Tennent, Rev. John C.	Chaplain	33d North Carolina Regiment	Glyndon, Md.
Terrell, George W.	Private	Co. B, 19th Virginia Regiment	1503 W. Lanvale St.
Terres, Charles E.	Lieutenant	5th North Carolina Cavalry	894 W. Baltimore St.
Thomas, D. L.	Private	Co. K, 1st Maryland Cavalry	329 N. Charles St.
Thomas, Joshua	Private	Headquarters A. N. V.	723 N. Carey St.
Thomas, J. Wm.	Sergeant	Co. H, 1st Maryland Infantry	122 Mosher St.
Thomas, George	Captain	Co. H, 1st Maryland Infantry	Mattaponi, St. Mary's Co., Md.
Thomas, Chas. C.	Private	Lathan's Battery.	
Thompson, John W.	Private	Co. G, 2d Maryland Infantry	Leonardstown, Md.
Thom, J. Pembroke	Captain	Co. C, Irish Battalion	826 Park Ave.
Thelin, Wm. T.	Private	Co. C, 2d Maryland Infantry	Mt. Washington.
Thorburn, H. C.	Captain	Fredericksburg Artillery	417 N. Charles Ss.

NAME.	RANK.	BRANCH OF SERVICE.	ADDRESS.
Thurston, James.	Lieutenant.	Marine Corps C. S. A.	19 W. Preston St.
Tinges, Chas. S.	Private.	4th Maryland Artillery.	233 W. Lafayette Ave.
Todd, Wm. H.	Private.	Co. C, 22d Maryland Cavalry.	Warren, Baltimore Co.
Tolson, Thomas H.	Lieutenant.	2nd Maryland Infantry.	1424 Argyle Ave.
Torsch, John W.	Captain.	Co. E, 2nd Maryland Infantry.	2002 E. Baltimore St.
Tompkins, Wm. T.	Private.	Co. C, 19th Virginia Infantry.	Carroll, Baltimore, Md.
Tonnay, S. C.	Private.	Co. E, 1st Maryland Infantry.	Towson, Baltimore Co.
Trapier, Theo. D.	Private.	Marion's Artillery.	
Travers, John M.	Private.	Gilnor's Battalion.	524 Mulberry St.
Trippe, Andrew C.	Lieutenant.	Ordnance Duty.	1522 Eutaw Place.
Trust, George.	Private.	Breathed Battery.	39 E. Hill St.
Tucker, E. Brison.	Ordnance Sergeant.	3rd Virginia Infantry.	2321 Madison Ave.
Tucker, George W.	Sergeant.	Co. F, 12th Virginia Cavalry.	Baltimore.
Tunis, Theophilus.	Private.	Co. B, 1st Maryland Cavalry.	Carrollton Hotel.
Turner, Benj.	Sergeant.	Co. C, 40th Virginia Infantry.	Baltimore.
Turner, Rev. J. H.	Lieutenant.	Co. K, 10th Virginia Cavalry.	Lutherville.
Turpin, Thomas L.	Private.	Gilnor's Battalion.	1666 W. Baltimore St.
Vaughman, John M.	Lieutenant.	Co. D, 10th Virginia Cavalry.	1027 N. Mount St.
Van Meter, R. B.	Private.	Co. F, 1st Virginia Cavalry.	1109 N. Mount St.
Virden, Wm. W., M. D.	Surgeon.	Confederate States Army.	Lapadum, Md.
Vogt, F. E.	Sergeant.	Co. F, 1st Maryland Infantry.	Atkin's Tank, Smyth Co., W. Va.
Wagner, Chas. V.	Private.	Co. G, 7th Virginia Cavalry.	
Wagoner, Henry E.	Private.	Co. D, 1st Tennessee Infantry.	Reisterstown, Md.
Waggner, Louis C.	Private.	Co. E, 61st Virginia Infantry.	430 N. Carey St.
Walker, Geo. W.	Assistant Engineer.	Confederate States Navy.	954 W. Franklin St.
Waller, Thaddeus W.	Corporal.	Co. K, 1st Georgia Infantry.	1609 McHenry St.
Wallis, H. C.	Sergeant.	Co. F, 1st Maryland Cavalry.	
Waller, Thos.	Colonel.	9th Virginia Cavalry.	
Walsh, John.	Private.	Graham's Battery.	1104 Mosher St.
Walter, John A.	Private.	Baltimore Light Artillery.	1509 Hanover St.
Walters, Wm. C.	Captain.	Col. Zarvonas Commanding.	2143 Penn. Ave.
Walter, Edward H.	Lieutenant.	Co. A, 1st Virginia Cavalry.	410 S. Payson St.
Ward, Frank X.	Captain.	Staff of Genl. Elzey.	1814 N. Charles St.
Ward, T. J., M. D.	Private.	Baltimore Light Artillery.	605 St. Paul St.

NAME.	RANK.	BRANCH OF SERVICE.	ADDRESS.
Warnick, John F.	Private	Lucas Battery	Washington, D. C.
Watkins, Nichols W.	Private	Baltimore Light Artillery	19 E. Saratoga St.
Watters, James D.	Lieutenant	Co. C, 1st Maryland Cavalry	Bel Air.
Watts, Philip	Private	Co. B, 35th Virginia Battalion	Pikesville, Md.
Watts, John N.	Private	Co. C, 2nd Maryland Infantry	Elkridge Landing.
Weaver, L. A.	Private	Co. B, 15th Virginia Cavalry	934 N. Stricker St.
Weems, Chas. H. Jr.	Private	Co. A, 2nd Maryland Cavalry	1207 Winchester St.
Webb, Otway G.	Private	Co. I, 40th Virginia Infantry	707 Scott St.
Weeks, Henry	Private	Co. D, 1st Maryland Infantry	723 N. Mount St.
Wegner, Henry L.	Private	Co. D, 1st Maryland Infantry	
Welch Edward A.	Corporal	Co. C, 2nd Maryland Infantry	
Welch, Robert H.	Private	Co. C, 2nd Maryland Infantry	Annapolis, Md.
Welsh, Warner G.	Captain	Co. D, 1st Maryland Cavalry	Liberty, Md.
Wells, John B.	Lieutenant	Co. A, 2nd Maryland Cavalry	935 W. Lexington St.
Wernsing, Henry	Private	Co. C, 15th Virginia Cavalry	802 Aisquith St.
West, Chas. N.	Private	Savannah Vol. Guards	1606 Bolton St.
West, N. G., M. D.	Surgeon	Ashby's Cavalry	Leesburg, Va.
West, John P.	Private	Co. G, 7th Virginia Cavalry	Petersville, Va.
Weston, Napoleon B.	Private	Co. A, Stark's Artillery	304 N. Central Ave.
Wharton, J. M.	Sergeant Major	21st Virginia Infantry	1529 Entaw Place.
Wheatley, Wm. F.	Corporal	Co. B, 2nd Maryland Infantry	1934 Mt. Royal Terrace.
Wheeler, Jas R.	Private	Co. E, 1st Maryland Cavalry	1022 Linden Ave.
Wheeler, S. W.	Private	Co. B, 19th Virginia Artillery	1105 Forrest Place.
Wheeler, Albert.	Private	2nd Maryland Artillery	779 W. Lexington St.
Wheeley, T. N.	Private	Co. B, 25th Virginia Battalion	1416 McElderry St.
Wheeley, J. Fountain	Private	Co. D, 1st Virginia Infantry	639 Ensor St.
White, J. McK.	Private	Co. A, 2nd Maryland Infantry	915 St. Paul St.
White, James H.	Private	Co. E, 19th Virginia Artillery	914 McDonough St.
Whiteley, Wm.	Private	Co. H, 17th Virginia Infantry	M. L. C. S. H.
Wickliffe, A. J.	Corporal	Richmond Reserves	2020 N. Calvert St.
Wigfall, Francis H.	Major	Staff of Gen'l Jos. E. Johnston	142 W. Lanvale St.
Wight, C. C.	Captain	31st Virginia Infantry	2519 Madison Ave.
Williams, F. J., M. D.	Lieutenant	Co. I, 31st N. C. Infantry	1114 S. Chesapeake St.
Williams, John Tyler	Private	Co. C, 12th Virginia Reg.	158 S. Sharp St.

NAME.	RANK.	BRANCH OF SERVICE.	ADDRESS.
Williams, Taylor	Private	20th Virginia Artillery	508 W. Preston St.
Williams, Z. F.	Sergeant	Breathed Battery	2233 N. Calvert St.
Williams, John P., Sr.	Private	Co. H, 1st Maryland Infantry	1503 W. Mulberry St.
Williams, R. A.	Major	Staff Duty	2109 St. Paul St.
Wills, James A.	Private	Co. B, 2d Maryland Infantry	Issue, Chas. Co., Md.
Wilson, Wm. B.	Private	Co. K, 1st Virginia Cavalry	1228 N. Charles St.
Wilson, Wm. A.	Sergeant	Co. B, 1st Maryland Cavalry	Baltimore.
Williams, John J., M. D.	Corporal	43rd Virginia Cavalry	726 N. Carey St.
Willison, Albert A.	Private	Co. G, 1st Virginia Cavalry	734 Gorsuch Ave.
Wilson, J. H.	Private	4th Maryland Artillery	415 W. Mulberry St.
Wilson, George W.	Private	1st Maryland Artillery	Upper Marlboro, P. G. Co., Md.
Wilson, J. J. W.	Lieutenant	Co. H, 23d Virginia Infantry	Washington, D. C.
Wilson, John A.	Passed Midshipman	C. S. Steamer Stonewall	
Wilson, Laucel	Private	Co. F, 2d Virginia Infantry	1515 Hull St.
Wilson, Dr. Pierce B.	Private	Co. H, 1st Georgia Reserves	620 W. North Ave.
Wilson, R. N.	Captain	Early's Brigade	305 W. Madison St.
Wilson, Samuel	1st Lieutenant	10th Va. Bat. Artillery	208 F. Biddle St.
Wilson, William Thomas	Private	Co. B, 3rd Virginia Battalion	123 N. Bond St.
Wilmer, Skipwith	Lieutenant	Staff, 1st Div, 2d Corps, A. N. V.	915 N. Charles St.
Wiltshire, J. G., M. D.	Lieutenant	Mosby's Cavalry	714 N. Howard St.
Windbigler, George H.	Private	Co. I, 10th Virginia Infantry	832 Columbia Ave.
Windsor, Richard B.	Major	Q. M. C. S. A.	716 Park Ave.
Windsor, C. Hall	Private	2d Co. Independent Signal Corps	1606 Edmondson Ave.
Wise, Henry A., Jr.	Captain	Co. A, Cades V. M. I.	421 Courtland St.
Wise, Henry A.	Private	Co. B, 2d Maryland Infantry	1404 W. Baltimore St.
Wissman, Louis B.	Private	Co. B, 1st Maryland Cavalry	Beltsville, P. G. Co., Md.
Withers, Douglas A.	Private	Co. G, 47th Virginia Infantry	M. L. C. S. H.
Wood, Chas. E.	Private	Co. L, 5th Virginia Infantry	9 St. Paul St.
Wood, George W.	Mil. Telegraph Operator	Co. D, Crescent, La., Regiment	1700 Eutaw Place.
Woodhouse. E. N.	Private	A. N. V.	M. L. C. S. H.
Woolsey, John	Private	Co. D, 8th Louisiana Infantry	1041 W. Mulberry St.
Wooldridge, R. A.	Private	Co. C, 9th Virginia Infantry	907 Park Ave.
Wortham, William G.	Com. Sergeant	Co. H, 55th Virginia Regiment	257 Dolphin Ave.
Worthington, Eugene	Private	1st Maryland Artillery	Annapolis, Md.

NAME.	RANK.	BRANCH OF SERVICE.	ADDRESS.
Wright, W. T.	Sergeant	Co. E, 50th Virginia Infantry	826 N. Gilmor St.
Wright, Daniel G.	Lieutenant	Co. D, 1st Virginia Regulars	142 W. Lanvale St.
Wright, O. H.	Private	Co. E, 30th Virginia Infantry	1326 Riggs Ave.
Wright, Solomon	Sergeant	Co. E, 1st Maryland Cavalry	1010 Milton Place.
Wysham, Wm. E., M. D.	Surgeon	Confederate States Navy	Cantonsville, Balto. Co., Md.
Yates, Thos. F.	Private	Co. K, 1st Virginia Cavalry	Leonardtown, Md.
Yeatman, Henry	A. Master	Confederate States Navy	2111 Jefferson Place.
Young, Benjamin	Private	4th Maryland Artillery	M. L. C. S. H.
Zeil, Robert R.	Private	Co. F, 7th Virginia Cavalry	2102 McCulloh St.
Zellers, John	Private	35th Virginia Cavalry	1417 E. Monument St.
Zinmers, Louis	Lieutenant	P. A. C. S.	
Zimmerman, Frank A.	Lieutenant	Co. B, 9th Virginia Infantry	2529 Mary St.
Zimmerman, Rev., Geo. H.	Chaplain	12th Virginia Cavalry	Easton, Md.

MALE DESCENDANTS.

NAME.	SON OF	ADDRESS.
Andrews, Geo Snowden	Lt.-Col. R. Snowden Andrews	107 W. North Ave.
Baker, Wm. W.	Private Henry Baker	Stevenson's, Balto. Co.
Blackford, W. R.	Col. Wm. W. Blackford	
Bowen, Henry T.	Private Henry B. Bowen	1114 Columbia Ave.
Biays, Tolley A.	Private Geo. Biays	318 Courtland St.
Briscoe, J N. D.	Private Henry Briscoe	Princess Anne, Md.
Briscoe, J. C.	Private Henry Briscoe	310 W. Madison St.
Bruce, W. Cabell	Capt. Chas. Bruce	1309 N. Calvert St.
Bussey, Thos. A.	Private J. T. Bussey	Huntsville, Ala.
Byrd, Jno. D.	Surgeon Harvey L. Byrd	1809 Park Ave.
Chambers, R. E.	Private R. M. Chambers, Jr	1514 John St.
Chambers, M. N.	Private R. M. Chambers, Jr	1514 John St.
Clinton, Thos. L.	Private H. Dewitt Clinton	224 S. Eden St.
Crabtree, Geo. W.	Private Albert P. Crabtree	101 W. Saratoga St.
Crone, Michael, Jr.	Private Michael Crone	211 W. Preston St.
Crouch, Junius P. M.	Private F. Nicholls Crouch	Penn & King Sts
Douglas, W. Bruce	Private R. F. Douglas	1656 N. Gilmor St.
Dunlap, James	Private Donald M. Dunlap	1120 N. Carrollton Ave.
Du Val, T E.	Private J. R. Du Val	1724 N. Charles St.
Essex, William	Q. M. Sergt. Geo. W. Essex	21 Fort Ave.
Eubank, Walter L.	Private Geo. W. Eubank	2222 Bank St.
Field, Chas. W.	Major-Gen. Chas. W. Field	Glenn Bldg., St. Paul St.
Fitzgerald, P. Morrison	Private W. H. Fitzgerald	1811 N. Charles St.
Gaither, A. Bradley	Capt. Geo. R. Gaither	17 E. 21st St.
Gaither, Chas. D.	Capt. Geo. R. Gaither	510 Cathedral St.
Gaither, Geo. R., Jr.	Capt. Geo. R. Gaither	602 Cathedral St.
Gaither, John D.	Capt. Geo. R. Gaither	510 Cathedral St.
Garrigues, J. Ralph	Private H. H. Garrigues	216 N. Carey St.
Grimes, Ashton	Major-Gen. Bryan Grimes	Grimesland, N. C.
Grimes, J. Bryan	Major-Gen. Bryan Grimes	Grimesland, N. C.
Hall, N. Ingraham	Major W. B. Hall	310 W. Hoffman St.
Hawks, A. W.	Major W. J. Hawks	1018 Hopkins Ave.

NAME.	GRANDSON OF	ADDRESS.
Hawks, J. Wells	Maj. W. J. Hawks	1018 Hopkins Ave.

NAME.	SON OF	ADDRESS.
Hoffman, J. T.	Private Geo. W. Hoffman	1306 McHenry St.
Hutton, Harry M.	Private Chas. C. Hutton	847 N. Eutaw St.
Jenkins, Frank C.	Private W. Kennedy Jenkins	307 E. Lanvale St.
Jenkins, Chas. K.	Private W. Kennedy Jenkins	307 E. Lanvale St.
Jeffords, Rob't J., Jr.	Col. Robt. J. Jeffords	323 St. Paul St.
Johnson, Bradley S.	Gen. Bradley T. Johnson	Georgetown, D. C.
Knox, Thos. P.	Sergeant Richard Knox	224 S. Collington Ave.

NAME.	SON OF	ADDRESS.
Lee, J. L. G.	Sergt-Major Otho S. Lee	Bel Air, Harford Co., Md.
Leland, J. W.	Lieutenant C. W. Leland	1704 Druid Hill Ave.
Lotz, Chas.	Private Michael Lotz	2324 E. Monument St.
Lotz, John	Private Michael Lotz	2104 E. Monument St.
Maloy, Wm. M	Private Wm. C. Maloy	1027 McCulloh St.
Marston, Jas. H	Sergeant Harry A. Marston	706 Portland St.
Maynadier, T. M	Private J. H. Maynadier	122 W. 20th St.
McCann, J. Edward	Private Wm. V. McCann	412 N. Paca St.
McNulty, Chas.	Capt. John McNulty	1312 Ensor St.
McNulty, Clifton	Capt. John McNulty	Fayette St. & Jackson Sq.
McKelvey, A. Lee	Sergeant Chas. N. McKelvey	1200 N. Gay St.
Mears, Rev. A. Deloser	Col. Gaston Mears	2935 Dillon St.
Minor, C. C	Sergeant C. C. Minor	1007 N. Mount St.
Orrick, H. A.	Capt. Johnson Orrick	1521 Bolton St.
Peters, Jas. Girvin	Lieutenant Winfield Peters	1117 McCulloh St.
Pilker, Wm. M.	Private M. Pilker	1020 Watson St.
Polk, Geo. Beach	Capt. Alexander H. Polk	3106 St. Paul St.
Ranson, H. W	Major A. R. H. Ranson	Catonsville, Balto. Co.
Redwood, Frank T	Private W. H. Redwood	P. O. Box 854, Baltimore.
Shields, John A	Private Owen Shields	1412 N. Central Ave.
Strahan, C. Merton	Lieutenant Chas. Strahan	Athens, Ga.
Sloan, Chas. W	Capt. John A. Sloan	1621 McCulloh St.
Smith, Chas. G.	Corporal Hamilton T. Smith	1733 Hollins St.
Staub, W. H.	Captain R. P. H. Staub	1407 Linden Ave.
Staub, J. Tegmeyer	Capt. R. P. H. Staub	1407 Linden Ave.
Stewart, Richard E.	Surgeon W. F. Stewart	213 N. Carey St.
Tabb, John, Jr.	Surgeon John Tabb	1724 N. Charles St.
Thelin, Elias Griswold	Private Wm. T. Thelin	Mt. Washington.

NAME.	GRANDSON OF	ADDRESS.
Trimble, Isaac R	Gen. Isaac R. Trimble	1123 N. Eutaw St.

NAME.	SON OF	ADDRESS.
Tyler, J. Harry	Sergeant Geo. Tyler	St. Louis, Mo.
Waller, C. H.	Corporal Thaddeus Waller	342 S. Calhoun St.
White, Elijah B.	Colonel E. V. White	31 W. Mt. Royal Ave.
Williams, J. P., Jr.	Private J. P. Williams	1503 W. Mulberry St.
Winder, Chas. Sydney	General Chas. Sydney Winder	Tunis Mills, Md.
Wroe, Philip W.	Lieutenant A. D. Wroe	1127 Bolton St.
Wroe, John C	Lieutenant A. D. Wroe	1127 Bolton St.
Wood, Benjamin H	Private Joseph T. Wood	1400 Cooksie St.
Winder, Ed. Lloyd	General Chas. F. Winder	33 S. Gay St.

AUXILIARY MEMBERS.

Chapman, W. J. .... 1533 Edmondson Ave ....
Dennis, James T. .... Princess Anne, Somerset Co., Md. ......
Durchhausen, F. Charles .... 1504 Baker St ....
Gray, John T. .... 715 N. Broadway ....
Gephart, John .... Mt. Washington, Baltimore Co., Md. ....
Graves, Roswell Woods .... 1015 Madison Ave ....
Hopkins, Lewis N. .... City Hall ....
McElroy, James W. .... 102 E. Lexington St ....
McAleese, Chas. J. .... City Hall ....
Marbury, Wm. H. .... 12 St. Paul St ....
Morse, Thos. W. .... 1017 N. Broadway ....
Magruder, Rob't .... Arlington, Baltimore Co., Md. ......
Oehm, Chas. H. .... 5 & 7 W. Baltimore St ....
Popplein, Frank .... 1709 Eutaw Place ....
Popplein, Andrew .... 1709 Eutaw Place ....
Ruby, Wm. H. .... Towson, Md. ....
Raynor, Isadore .... 1412 Eutaw Place ....
Sans, Conway W. .... 624 N. Gilmor St ....
Scharf, W. J. .... 819 Fremont Ave ....
Tarleton, James R. .... 315 N. Carey St ....
Tylor, Henry Leigh .... 105 W. Lanvale St ....
Walters, Edwin .... 35 S. Gay St ....
Warfield, Edwin .... 7 N. Calvert St ....
Waters, John .... 1704 N. Charles St ....

HONORARY MEMBERS.

LIEUT. GENL. WADE HAMPTON,

GENL. LORD WOLSELEY,
Adjutant General British Army.

DECEASED MEMBERS

OF THE

SOCIETY OF THE

Army and Navy of the Confederate States

IN THE STATE OF MARYLAND.

Deceased Members.

Name.	Rank.	Branch of Service.
Adams, Henry S.	Private	Co. E, 1st Maryland Infantry.
Addison, John W.	Sergeant	Co. F, 2nd Virginia Infantry.
Allan, Wm.	Lieutenant Colonel	Ordnance Department, A. N. V.
Baldwin John H.	Lieutenant	Co. A, 1st Virginia Battalion.
Barry, Wm. J.	Surgeon	P. A. C. S.
Beale, L. W.	Corporal	Co. D, 3rd Virginia Infantry.
Beall, E. Sinclair	Sergeant Major	Otey Battery.
Bester, J. Rolin	Private	Co. I, 19th Virginia cavalry.
Beucke, Chas. L.	Private	Baltimore Light Infantry.
Bishop, Geo. W.	Sergeant Major	1st Maryland Infantry.
Billopp, Thos. F.	Captain	29th Georgia Infantry.
Blackistone, S. H.	Private	Co. A, 1st Maryland Cavalry.
Blumenauer, Mich.	Private	1st Maryland Artillery.
Brattan, John L.	Lieutenant	Co. A, 1st N. C. Infantry.
Breed, L. H.	Private	Co. F, 1st Maryland Cavalry.
Brennen, Wm.	Sergeant	Ward's Battery.
Brown, J. R. Jr.	Private	Co. A, 1st Maryland Cavalry.
Buchanan, J. Rowan	Private	1st Maryland Artillery.
Buck, R. B.	Lieutenant	Co. B, 17th Virginia Infantry.
Byrd, Dr. Harvey L.	Surgeon	Confederate States Army.
Carter, John P.	Lieutenant	30th Virginia Infantry.
Chilcutt, Joshua	Private	Co. D, 2nd Maryland Infantry.
Corkey, S. S.	Private	Co. A, 1st Maryland Cavalry.
Codd, Wm. H.	Chief Engineer	Confederate States Navy.
Cole Wm. H., M. D.	Surgeon	Confederate States Army.
Coleman, H. Eaton	Colonel	12th N. C. Infantry.
Cook, Wm. S.	Private	Co. E, 5th Virginia Cavalry.
Crask, Seldon F.	Private	Co. C, 9th Virginia Cavalry.
Cullingsworth, R.	Private	Co. H, 17th Virginia Infantry.
Dallam, H. Clay	Private	Genl. Elzey's Command.
Dallam, Wm. W.	Lieutenant	1st Engineers, A. N. V.
Darden, Frank W.	Private	43d Virginia Battalion.
Davison, Thos. H.	Sergeant	Co. E, 1st Maryland Infantry.
Ditty, C. Irving	Captain	Co. F, 1st Maryland Cavalry.
Doherty, Charles	Sergeant	Corps Sharp Shooters, A. N. V.
Dolan, Patrick H.	Sergeant	Co. C, 1st Maryland Cavalry.
Dorsey, Wm. H. B.	Lieutenant	Co. D, 1st Maryland Cavalry.
Downing, Sam'l	Captain	Co. I, 55th Virginia Infantry.
Du Barry W. D.	Private	27th S. C. Infantry.
Duval, Ferdinand	Captain	2nd Maryland Infantry.
Dickinson, Geo. C.	Captain	Eng. A. N. V.
Douglas, Hugh T.	Captain	Co. F, 1st Reg. Eng.
Dammington, Vir. G.	Private	Co. B, 2nd Virginia Cavalry.
Dorsey, Ezekiel S.	Sergeant	2nd Maryland Infantry.
Edmonds, John J.	Private	Co. C, 47th N. C. Infantry.
Ellis, John	Private	Co. D, 28th Mississippi Cavalry.
Emory Dan'l Grant	Private	Co. C, 1st Maryland Cavalry.
Exo, Chas. E.	Private	Co. D, 1st Maryland Infantry.

NAME.	RANK.	BRANCH OF SERVICE.
Essex, Geo. W	Sergeant	Walker's Battalion.
Evans, Charles A	Sergeant Major	Pelham's Batalion.
Ezell, Malachia	Private	13th Miss. Infantry.
Fahey, Alexander A.	Private	Courier for General R. E. Lee.
Febrey, Moses A.	Lieutenant	Breathed's Battery.
Fisher, Charles W.	Private	Kevill's Battery.
Fitzgerald, W. B.	Private	1st Virginia Cavalry.
Foley, Rich. Fleming	Captain	Confederate States Navy.
Gardner, I. de Barth	Sergeant	Robinson's Artillery.
Garnett, R. A	Sergeant	Co. C, 51st Virginia Infantry.
Garrigues, H. H.	Private	Co. C, 14th Tennessee Infantry.
Garrison, H. T.	Private	Co. A, 9th Virginia Cavalry
Gatch, J. A. Ross	Private	Cobb's Kentucky Battery.
Gavin, Michael F.	Private	Co. K, 12th Virginia Infantry.
Giles, Wm. Fell, Jr.	Private	Co. C, 1st Maryland Cavalry.
Gilmor, Harry	Lieutenant Colonel.	Gilmor's Cavalry.
Gilmor, Hoffman.	Private	Gilmor's Cavalry.
Griswold, Elias	Major.	Prov. Mar., Richmond, Va.
Goolrick, Dr., P.	Assistant Surgeon.	Pegram's Brigade.
Groves, Thomas F.	Private	Co. B, 2d Maryland Infantry.
Hackney, B. S.	Private	34th Virginia Infantry.
Hall, W. Carvel,	Major and A. A. G.	Maj. Gen. Isaac R. Trimble's Staff.
Hall, Martin Y.	Sergeant	Co. A, 31st Virginia Infantry.
Hancock, Hartwell P.	Corporal	Co. D, 14th Virginia Infantry.
Hanley, Thomas J.	Private	Co. G, 1st Maryland Infantry.
Harris, E. H.	Major & Quarterm.	O. Alabama Infantry.
Haynes, James A.	Captain	Co. K, 55th Virginia Infantry.
Herbert, James R.	Lieutenant Colonel.	2d Maryland Infantry.
Herzog, J. Lewis.	Sergeant	Moorehead's Rangers.
Hoffman, John.	Private	43rd Virginia Battalion.
Hollins, George N.	Commodore	Confederate States Navy.
Holland, John R.	Private	1st Virginia Cavalry.
Holland, Michael.	Private	6th Virginia Infantry.
Hollyday G. T. of W.	Private	35th Virginia cavalry.
Howard, Dr. E. Lloyd	Surgeon	A. N. V.
Howard, George	Lieutenant	22th Virginia Infantry.
Ingraham, Duncan.	Flag Officer	Confederate States Navy.
Jackson, E. J.	Captain	22d Virginia Infantry.
James, Alfred R.	Lieutenant	Co. D, 28th Virginia Infantry.
Jeffers, Wm. H.	Private	Co. B, 1st Maryland Cavalry.
Jones, Samuel	Major General	Confederate States Army.
Jones, Wm. F.	Assistant Engineer.	Confederate States Navy.
Jordon, John R	Chief Engineer.	Confederate States Navy.
Kaelcher, John	Private	1st Virginia Infantry.
Keim, Charles W.	Captain	Confederate States Navy.
Kemp, Thomas F.	Corporal	Co. C, 5th Virginia Cavalry.
Kennon, Beverly.	Lieutenant	Confederate States Navy.
Kettlewell, Sam'l H.	Private	13th Virginia Infantry.
Knauff, George W.	Private	Co. D, 1st Maryland Cavalry.
Knowles, Raymond	Sergeant	Co. B, 62d Alabama Infantry.
Lane, Benjamin	Private	Co. A, 30th Virginia Infantry.
Latham, J. W.	Corporal	Co. F, 1st Maryland Cavalry.
Lattimore, C. W.	Color Sergeant	40th Virginia Infantry.
Lear, Alpheus	Sergeant	17th Virginia Infantry.
Lewis, George B.	Sergeant	Co. H, 6th Virginia Infantry.
Linthicum, Edwin.	Private	Co. A, 1st Maryland Cavalry.
Lutts, Jno. J.	Lieutenant	Co. E, 1st Maryland Infantry.
Mackall, Leonard C.	Private	Co. C, 1st Maryland Cavalry.
Magruder, Edw. W.	Private	Co. E, 1st Maryland Cavalry.

NAME.	RANK.	BRANCH OF SERVICE.
Mahool, Thomas,	Captain	3d Georgia Infantry.
Mallon, Henry B.	Private	Co. A, 1st Maryland Infantry.
Marston, Fred A.	Corporal	Baltimore Light Artillery.
Marston, Harry A.	Sergeant	2d Maryland Artillery.
Martin, Wm. D.	Lieutenant	Co. A, Lucas Battalion.
Mason, John T.	Surgeon	Confederate States Navy.
Mauphin, R. W.	Midshipman	C. S. Steamer Patrick Henry.
Maury, J. S.	Lieut. Commanding	Confederate States Navy.
McBlair, Charles H.	Commodore	Confederate States Navy.
McGuire, Charles E.	Sergeant	Co. A, 2d Maryland Infantry.
Miller, John H.	Private	Co. B, 40th Virginia Infantry.
Michael, John W.	Private	Co. C, 2d Maryland Infantry.
Miller, Howard.	Private	Co. B, 40th Virginia Infantry.
Moore, J. D.	Captain	Huger's Artillery.
Monk, Christopher.	Private	Co. E, 1st Maryland Cavalry.
Moore, Philip I.	Sergeant-Major.	1st Maryland Infantry.
Murray, Ed. C.	Private	Co. E, 1st Maryland Cavalry.
Maddox, Martin.	Private	Co. A, Mosby's Cavalry.
Norvell, Edward.	Lieutenant.	Otey Battery.
Ohlgard, Philip.	Private	2d Maryland Infantry.
Pagoud, Joseph S.	Private	Jefferson Mounted Guards.
Patrick, James T.	Private	Co. G, 1st Maryland Infantry.
Pearce, John F.	Private	Co. E, 1st Maryland Infantry.
Peerce, John T.	Private	Steuart's Horse Artillery.
Peddicord, C. A. L.	Private	Co. B, 3d Virginia Cavalry.
Perkins, Livius C.	Private	Co. F, 2d North Carolina Cavalry.
Perrie, Thomas H.	Private.	Co. B, 1st Maryland Cavalry.
Peters, Geo. Henry.	Private	Co. G, 3d Virginia Reserve Forces.
Perkins, John W.	Sergeant.	Co. E, 41st Virginia Infantry.
Porter, Hugh.	Private	Co. A, 1st Maryland Infantry.
Potter, Hugh.	Private	13th Virginia Infantry.
Prout, John W.	Sergeant.	Co. D, 2d Maryland Infantry.
Preece, Edward V.	Private	Co. C, 1st Maryland Infantry.
Porter, Wallace D.	Private.	Richmond Howitzers.
Register, Dr. Wils'nG	Private.	Baltimore Light Artillery.
Ridgely, John.	Color Sergeant.	1st Maryland Cavalry.
Roberts, Jos. K.	Lieutenant	Co. E, 1st Maryland Cavalry.
Robey, Townley	Sergeant	Co. E, 1st Maryland Cavalry.
Robinson Henry	Major	General Longstreet's Staff.
Robinson, John M.	Captain	Staff General Longstreet.
Rohr, Charles.	Private.	Weems' Cavalry.
Ross, Geo. L.	Sergeant	Co. G, 1st Maryland Infantry.
Rhett, Thos. G.	Lieutenant Colonel.	Artillery.
Rowe, James F.	Private.	Co. E, 5th Virginia Cavalry.
Rowland, Thomas	Major and A. A. G.	General Ransom's Staff.
Ruff, G. Fred.	Sergeant.	Co. D, 1st Maryland Infantry.
Rhett, Thos. S.	Colonel	Confederate States Army.
Schoolfield, L. H.	Private.	Baltimore Light Artillery.
Schwartzman, G. A.	Major and A. A. G.	Staff of General G. W. C. Lee.
Scott, Channing N.	Sergeant	Co. B, 2d Maryland Cavalry.
Selden, W. A.	Sergeant.	Marine Signal Corps.
Severe John O	Private.	Co. I, 59th Virginia Infantry.
Shearer, Geo. M	Lieutenant	Co. A, 1st. Maryland Infantry.
Shellman, Geo. K.	Lieutenant	Co. A, 1st Maryland Infantry.
Sims, John.	Private	Co. B, 2d Maryland Cavalry.
Smith, E. T.	Private	Co. K, 9th Virginia Cavalry.
Smith, Wm. H.	Sergeant.	Co. A, 2d Maryland Infantry.
Smith, Seabory D.	Private.	2d Maryland Artillery.
Solano, P. G.	Sergeant Major.	5th Florida Infantry.

NAME.	RANK.	BRANCH OF SERVICE.
Staylor, Geo. W.	Private	2d Maryland Artillery.
Steele, John	Private	Co. D, 1st Maryland Cavalry.
Stewart, Joseph H.	Major	Confederate States Army.
Steuart, W. F.	Surgeon	Confederate States Army.
Stout, W. C.	Private	2d Maryland Artillery.
Strobel, R. S.	Sergeant	Co. D, 27th South Carolina Infantry.
Stroemer, Alphonso.	Bugler	2d Georgia Artillery.
Thomas, Raleigh C.	Private	Co. C, 1st Maryland Cavalry.
Thomas, Edwin	Private	Co. B, 1st Maryland Cavalry.
Thompson, D. B'y.	Captain and A. A. G.	Staff of Genl. Wharton.
Thompson, C. G.	Captain	Ordnance Department.
Thompson, W. S.	Chief Engineer	Confederate States Navy.
Thompson, Dr. I. D.	Surgeon	Genl. Early's Command.
Todd, Joseph	Hospital Steward.	Confederate States Army.
Tolby, Geo. W.	Private	Co. A, 1st Maryland Cavalry.
Tolson, Albert	Private	1st Maryland Battery.
Trapier, Pierre, D.G.	Engineer Corps	Confederate States Army.
Trimble, Isaac R.	Major General	Division 1st Corps A. N. V.
Upshur, Levin	Sergeant	Gilmor's Battalion.
Waddell, James J.	Lieut. Commanding.	C. S. Steamer Shenandoah.
Waddell, James A.	Sergeant	Co. B, 23rd Virginia Infantry.
Walbrach, John J. B.	Lieutenant	Confederate States Army.
Walls; Dr. J. Wm.	Surgeon	Stonewall Brigade.
Waring, W. H.	Corporal	Co. F, 3d Virginia Cavalry.
Watkins, Louis J.	Private	Co. A, 1st Maryland Cavalry.
Weber, Edward	Private	Co. E, 1st Maryland Infantry.
Weems, James N.	Private	1st Maryland Artillery.
Wentworth, Geo. W.	Sergeant	Co. C, 2nd Maryland Infantry
Wharton, Wm. F.	Private	Co. C, 1st Maryland Cavalry.
Whilden, De Leon	Private	Walter Light S. C. Battery.
Williams, Thos. B. Jr.	Private	Co. C, 1st Maryland Cavalry.
Williamson, Jno. B.	Private	McNeal's Cavalry.
Wilkinson, John	Lieut. Commanding.	Confederate States Navy.
Willis, Z. L. C.	Captain	Co. B, 19th Virginia Artillery.
Wilson, James W.	Private	Co. B, 25th Virginia Infantry.
Woolfolk, James	Captain	Woolfolk's Battery.
Zollinger, Wm. P.	Lieutenant	Co. A, 2nd Maryland Infantry.

AUXILIARY MEMBERS.—DEAD.

FREDERICK RAINE.
E. CALVIN WILLIAMS.

HONORARY MEMBERS.—DEAD.

HON. JEFFERSON DAVIS,
Ex-President Confederate States of America.

www.ingramcontent.com/pod-product-compliance
Lightning Source LLC
Chambersburg PA
CBHW031406270326
41929CB00010BA/1352